FREEDOM AND INDOCTRINATION IN EDUCATION

Available in the Cassell Education series:

Freedom and Indoctrination in Education

International Perspectives

Edited by
Ben Spiecker and
Roger Straughan

CASSELL

Cassell Educational Limited
Villiers House
41/47 Strand
London WC2N 5JE, England

387 Park Avenue South
New York, NY 10016–8810, USA

First published 1991

British Library Cataloguing in Publication Data
Freedom and indoctrination in education:
   international perspectives.
   1. Education related to politics and sociology
   I. Spiecker, Ben *1943–*   II. Straughan, Roger *1941–*
   370.19
   ISBN 0–304–32481–7
      0–304–32441–8 pbk

Library of Congress Cataloging-in-Publication Data
Applied for
ISBN 0–304–32481–7
      0–304–32441–8 pbk

Typeset by Selectmove Ltd, London
Printed and bound in Great Britain by
Dotesios, Trowbridge, Wilts.

Contents

The Editors and Contributors

Robin Barrow, Faculty of Education, Simon Fraser University, Burnaby, BC.

Attila Horvath, Centre for School Development, National Institute of Education, Budapest.

Tasos Kazepides, Faculty of Education, Simon Fraser University, Burnaby, BC.

Jürgen Oelkers, Pädagogisches Institut, Universität Bern.

Harvey Siegel, Department of Philosophy, University of Miami, Coral Gables.

Ben Spiecker, Department of Education, Free University, Amsterdam.

Jan Steutel, Department of Education, Free University, Amsterdam.

Roger Straughan, Faculty of Education and Community Studies, University of Reading.

John White, Institute of Education, University of London.

John Wilson, Department of Educational Studies, University of Oxford.

Introduction

Freedom and indoctrination have proved to be topics of perennial interest to all concerned with education and upbringing. This is probably because the two concepts lie at the heart of the two most fundamental questions that can be asked about education—'What should be taught?' and 'How should it be taught?' The first question is about principles of selection—on what grounds should certain material be accepted or rejected as the subject matter of education, and who should make these choices? The second question is about principles of methodology—on what grounds should certain methods of teaching, child-rearing and learning be accepted or rejected?

Neither question can properly be considered without reference to the issues surrounding indoctrination and freedom and to the further complex problems which they pose. Is certain material, for example, to be excluded as non-educational if it contains 'doctrines' or 'theories' of a non-falsifiable kind? Does all religious, moral and political teaching fall into this category, or do further distinctions need to be drawn? Are the teacher's and parent's intentions an essential factor in determining what should be taught and how it should be taught? Are teachers the best people to make decisions about subject matter and methods, or if not who else should be consulted? Does any form of education or child-rearing necessarily involve some degree of indoctrination or some limitation of freedom? These are but a few of the questions tackled by the contributors to this book.

If indoctrination and freedom, however, have already received considerable attention from writers on education, why do we need this addition to the existing literature on the subject? Much of the previous work, particularly on indoctrination, has been purely analytical, and while it is essential to continue refining the analysis of the concepts under discussion (as several of the earlier chapters try to do) this task is most usefully seen as a necessary preliminary to further educational debate rather than an end in itself. Indoctrination and freedom in education pose moral as well as conceptual questions, which arise and are exemplified in particular historical, social and political contexts, and it is especially here that this book tries to add a new dimension to the debate. The contributors are drawn from a variety of cultural, academic and educational traditions, and this international representation has broadened and enriched the discussion by presenting and contrasting different approaches to freedom and indoctrination from the perspectives of these different traditions.

Until recently the communication and exchange of ideas between philosophers of education of the different continents was rather limited. This could be explained by the language barriers, by the divergent philosophical traditions or by the repressive influence the different political systems had on educational thinking. Current developments in Europe, however, have pointed the way to possibilities of increased dialogue and collaboration, in the light of the inevitable effects that these developments will have on educational systems and institutions. We hope that this book may help to play a modest part in furthering this dialogue.

The book falls roughly into two parts, the earlier chapters dealing specifically with the issue of indoctrination and the later ones exploring various aspects of freedom in education. Yet in almost all chapters where indoctrination is the central issue a link with freedom is made, while in those chapters that take freedom as a central topic, a connection with indoctrination is often brought to the fore.

In the opening chapter Tasos Kazepides argues that the Catholic church will last for many centuries because it has one of the most sophisticated programmes of indoctrination. For Kazepides indoctrination has a 'success' sense and can be explicated only in terms of doctrines and doctrinal beliefs regardless of the intentions of the indoctrinator. Passing on doctrines is to be distinguished from passing on scientific theories *as if* they were doctrines—that is, deliberately omitting the grounds for holding these beliefs. In order to reject the claim that the term 'doctrine' is vague and hence cannot be a necessary condition of indoctrination, Kazepides explores the conditions of (the hard view of) 'doctrine'. His analysis shows that doctrines are to be distinguished from the foundations of rationality, which Wittgenstein called the 'river-bed' or the 'unmoving foundations' of all our thoughts, judgements, language and actions. The latter will enable children to think, while the former act as stoppers that control thought and repress critical thinking.

The view that doctrinal beliefs are a necessary condition of 'indoctrination' is also defended by Ben Spiecker. But contrary to Kazepides, this philosopher of education conceives indoctrination also in a task sense. In addition to doctrines, intention is a second condition, for indoctrination is the deliberate attempt to still the development of a critical attitude, in particular the intellectual virtues and rational emotions. Doctrines have great potential to suppress critical dispositions and consequently questions concerning the validity of beliefs. After explaining Kohlberg's view on indoctrination, Spiecker argues that in moral indoctrination the question of the normative validity of social rules, conventions and prescriptions is systematically evaded, and that the term 'brainwashing' is better reserved for the breaking down of already developed critical dispositions (of adults).

For Harvey Siegel intentions, methods and content (doctrines) are neither necessary nor sufficient conditions for 'indoctrination'. In his 'results' or 'upshot' view of indoctrination, it is the non-evidential or non-critical style of belief which is the hallmark of indoctrination. Siegel distinguishes indoctrination from non-indoctrinative belief inculcation; in the latter, beliefs are held without rational justification, but can be redeemed by reasons if the believer is open to reason. In the case of indoctrination the believer has a non-evidential style of belief and his beliefs are not redeemable. Consequently early belief and habit inculcation is not indoctrinative, so long as the beliefs and habits enhance the child's rationality, and foster an evidential style of belief. Unlike Kazepides and Spiecker, for Siegel no specific sort of belief, be it religious or scientific, is excluded from the possibility of indoctrination.

Drawing on his personal experiences as the son of a minister of the Church of England, John Wilson strongly resists any attempt to dilute religious environments or traditions, particularly for the pseudo-reasons that they are 'indoctrinatory' or 'authoritarian'. From a Christian tradition one can gain a feeling of security, experience joy from corporate worship and acquire a general insight into what religion is about. According to Wilson the central religious questions are about the appropriateness of certain attitudes and emotions, particularly the attitude of worship towards certain objects. Philosophical problems about freedom and indoctrination will not worry us any longer when we understand that in religion, just as in morality, politics, aesthetics and other forms of thought and experience, two forms of commitment are required. In any religious education pupils have to become committed both to a particular religious tradition ('content') and to the impartial questioning and analysing of religious beliefs ('form').

Attila Horvath's contribution acts as a bridge between the earlier chapters, which focus upon indoctrination, and the later ones, which consider aspects of freedom. Examining freedom and indoctrination from an Eastern European perspective, Horvath reveals that these concepts have not featured explicitly in the educational systems of that area—indeed, there is no Hungarian word for 'indoctrination'. He offers an analysis of Marxist-Leninist conceptions of freedom and shows why these were not linked directly to theories of education. Indoctrination is interpreted as 'the deliberate action of changing and increasing the number of unquestioned things in a given culture', and is thus distinguished from merely traditional, static teaching. If the educational systems of Eastern Europe were really indoctrinatory, asks Horvath, how could the recent stunning changes have occurred?

Both Steutel and Oelkers take as their starting point the paradox between freedom and education: how can freedom be cultivated when constraining the child is inevitable? Jan Steutel tries to answer this question by tracing some conceptual relations between moral discipline and three forms of freedom. His analysis shows moral discipline to be a way of fostering the internalization of moral rules. Referring to his own upbringing in a Dutch neo-Calvinist milieu, Steutel argues that there is a negative connection between discipline and one form of freedom, animal freedom: discipline is an attempt to prevent the child from practising certain inclinations. A positive connection is revealed between discipline and autarchic freedom. A person is free in this sense of the word when he is motivated by a normative conception of life to which he gives his own assent. According to Steutel, the typical exponents of the neo-Calvinist subculture were such autarchic persons. In addition to autarchy, the morally autonomous person has the ability and tendency to think critically about the validity of moral rules (in Wilson's terms, he is also committed to the moral form). There is a neutral connection between this form of freedom and moral discipline. Grounding their religious–moral rules in the commanding will of God, the neo-Calvinists were not morally autonomous.

Jürgen Oelkers discusses two possible ways out of Kant's paradox of education and freedom, namely liberal education and child-centred education. In his research on the history of educational ideas, Oelkers traces the roots of liberal education in the eighteenth century. In this tradition two options are distinguished, letting the inner genius grow or forming customs and habits. Child-centred or progressive education claims that education is helping the soul to develop. The notion of soul is of Christian origin, and was revitalized by the Romantic movement. The adoption of the notion of the soul's free and natural development implies that education is nothing but indoctrination. Oelkers criticizes Neill's conception of progressive education on several points and concludes that liberal education, when it promotes understanding, is not necessarily indoctrination.

Can autonomy as an educational aim be justified? This is the question that John White tackles. Here again the distinction between the autarchic and the autonomous person is a vital one. Is it possible to look for a justification of personal autonomy of a universal type that is a necessary feature of personal well-being or human flourishing, or is it a particular ideal of the good life in a non-tradition-directed society? White distinguishes between a weaker and a stronger sense of personal autonomy. In order to flourish we must be personally autonomous in the weak sense, that is, make choices in our lives within the framework of existing institutions and conventions (for example marriage arrangements, jobs). Autonomy in the stronger sense requires critical reflectiveness about these basic social structures. Personal well-being or flourishing can be conceived in both a highly individualistic and in a wider or altruistic way. In the latter case, it is a part of my flourishing that I promote the well-being of friends and strangers. White argues that in our kind of open society the wider conception of well-being must prevail and that reflectiveness, and therefore strong autonomy, is unavoidable.

Developing the human mind and cultivating understanding requires freedom to express ideas, and therefore Robin Barrow rejects any censorship in schools. Barrow stresses the distinction between censorship and the broader term, selection. In censorship the suppression and alteration of material is based on criteria extraneous to that material, whereas in selection internal criteria are used. So schools are guilty of censorship in so far as they reject material for political or ideological reasons. The pursuit of the truth cannot advance without challenge and interplay of ideas and consequently, in principle, any expression should be legitimate, even if it is offensive. Barrow's conclusion neatly sums up what is a major theme of this book: schools have to accept Mill's argument that freedom of thinking is indispensable, particularly in enabling human beings to attain the mental stature of which they are capable.

Chapter 1

Religious Indoctrination and Freedom[1]

Tasos Kazepides

Philosophers of education who are interested in justifying religious indoctrination usually adopt one of the following two strategies. The first strategy is to take as the central use of education the one that refers to a person's upbringing and life experiences as in the phrase 'The education of Mikhail Gorbachev'. This sense of education includes all the learning and experiences that have shaped a person's mind and character regardless of their value—it is what sociologists refer to as the socialization of the individual. Since 'education' in this sense is an all-inclusive descriptive term, there are no values specific to it, and it now may include indoctrination and all other forms of miseducation.

It is difficult to see how such a broad view of education can be of any value to educational theorists, planners or practitioners since it is a chameleonic concept that merely reflects the preferences of the individual or the values of the prevailing group within a society. One of the consequences of holding this concept of education is that we have to abandon the belief that there are values specific to education and consequently the things we can say about education. We can no longer talk, for example, about educational or miseducational practices, programmes, institutions or policies and we cannot continue to talk about educational issues, problems or reasons. A concept of education that excludes nothing cannot be taken seriously in educational theorizing and planning because it offers no direction to our thinking and no guidance to our actions. Only educators with programmatic intentions or politicians who do not know better or who are afraid of alienating their supporters might resort to such vague definitions of our most fundamental concept.

The second strategy of the proponents of religious indoctrination is more subtle and sophisticated but equally unwarranted, confused and programmatic. They refuse to accept that the primary locus of indoctrination is religion, they maintain that the meaning of 'doctrine' is hopelessly vague and intractable, that doctrines are as common in science as they are in religion and that the criterion of whether a person is indoctrinating is not the doctrinal beliefs that are being inculcated but the miseducative methods or intentions of the teacher.

In this chapter I shall argue that all the above claims are false, that indoctrination is but *one* form of miseducation which must be distinguished from other forms such as propaganda or the teaching of prejudices and false or unjustified beliefs, that it can be explicated only in terms of doctrinal beliefs which are religious or quasi-religious (intention being parasitic on doctrines); that there are no such doctrines in science,[2] and that the questionable methods used by the indoctrinator together with his or her intentions presuppose specific doctrines that are being inculcated. Finally, I shall attempt to show that religious indoctrination puts severe constraints on our freedom of thought and is one of the most powerful enemies of the open society.

THE CONTEXT AND THE PROBLEM OF INDOCTRINATION

When philosophers argue that we ought to examine the various uses of words in their actual contexts, they do not mean that we must consult our dictionaries and enumerate all the various uses of the word we want to clarify (Strawson, 1963, p. xiii). Although such practices may be useful for other purposes they do not settle any philosophical questions; indeed they very often bring forth linguistic skeletons from bygone ages that add further confusion to the subject under examination. What philosophers have in mind is the study and explication of current linguistic usage (Austin, 1961, pp. 130–3). If words are tools then we must examine our tools in order to find out what actual work they perform in our language today, and for what purposes. It might be worth exploring the reasons why in the Middle Ages the word 'indoctrination' was used interchangeably with 'teaching', but that enquiry will not clarify our concept of indoctrination today—in fact it presupposes such clarification.

Our concern about indoctrination stems, first, from our commitment to education and the specific epistemological constraints that our concept of education imposes on various activities, programmes and institutions. In other words, education implies knowledge and understanding and therefore rules out superstitions, prejudices, doctrines, false beliefs, and the like. Our second reason is that while indoctrinated people are unwilling or incapable of subjecting their doctrinal beliefs to public rational scrutiny, most of them nonetheless want their doctrines to function as regulative principles of the way of life of the whole community. It is obvious, then, that indoctrination continues to be a very serious political problem in the modern world.

The paradigm cases of indoctrination are to be found within religious communities and institutions. The ordinary uses of 'indoctrination' suggest that it has to do with the transmission or inculcation of doctrinal beliefs. Indoctrination does not imply a specific activity or activities but conformity to some specific beliefs and rules that are at the foundations of a particular ideology. Just as we educate people by teaching them the humanities, the sciences and the arts, we indoctrinate people by teaching them particular doctrines. The difference between education and indoctrination lies in the nature of the criteria employed. Whereas for education they have to do with worthwhile knowledge and understanding according to intersubjective criteria, in the case of indoctrination they are wholly dependent on the nature of the parochial doctrines that are being inculcated. Ayatollahs, evangelists and bishops are not interested in indoctrination-in-general, because there is no such thing, but in the inculcation of specific doctrines that are foundational to their respective ways of life. The prepositional modifiers *into* and *with*, which accompany ordinary uses of the verb 'to indoctrinate', suggest that the doctrinal beliefs must be specific. Thus one indoctrinates the young into the doctrines of a particular church or with the doctrines of a religious ideology. In this respect 'indoctrinating *into* or *with*' behaves like 'training *in*': in both cases the prepositions limit the scope of their respective activities and specify their limited objectives.

Successful indoctrination results in the acceptance of doctrinal beliefs and commitment to them, whereas successful educational engagements aim at some worthwhile understanding. If a student, after careful consideration, rejects the doctrines he has been taught, the indoctrinator has failed in his or her task. On the other hand, if a student, after critical examination, rejects a scientific claim that he is being taught we do not say that the teacher has failed as an educator—in fact, if the student's rejection is based on rational grounds, we might even conclude that this episode was a paradigm case of educative teaching.

INDOCTRINATION AND INTENTIONS

Most existing discussions of indoctrination fail to provide a clear demarcation of the concept either because they fail to identify the correct criterion of indoctrination or, when they do, they do not succeed in describing it correctly. In the first category are those who take intention or method to be the criterion, while in the second are those who consider content to be the criterion of indoctrination.

Of the first two criteria, intention is the stronger candidate as it is on the basis of people's intentions that we characterize their actions—not merely on the basis of some behavioural descriptions of what they do. In most cases where we talk of a teacher indoctrinating students we refer to an intentional activity. The intention, however, always presupposes certain doctrines that are being inculcated. In the absence of doctrines there cannot be intention to indoctrinate. Just as 'teaching' implies a triadic relationship between the teacher, the student and what is to be taught, indoctrination implies a similar relationship between the indoctrinator, the student and doctrines. In fact this relationship is stricter in the case of indoctrinating than it is in the case of teaching. In ordinary language we talk about the 'self-taught' person but not about the 'self-indoctrinated' one. In the first case the teacher and the pupil are one and the same person while in the case of indoctrination an external indoctrinator is presupposed. The reason for this discrepancy has to do with the nature of doctrines. Self-taught people are those who have discovered certain truths or new ways of doing things, have developed certain skills or cultivated better tastes, have improved their methods of doing things or discovered new ones. All these things they acquired by trial and error, by following certain rules, by avoiding pitfalls and blind alleys, by correcting their errors and applying new techniques. For all these achievements self-taught people make use of public criteria, standards, rules, procedures and tests. All these achievements come up to certain public standards they can satisfy. What could it possibly mean to talk of the discovery of the doctrine of the infallibility of the Pope or of the *filioque* (the belief that the Holy Ghost proceeds from the Son, as well as from the Father)?

A second reason for rejecting the intention criterion of indoctrination is that it is of little use for educational planning. A philosophical examination of indoctrination should offer the educational community a clearly demarcated concept that can be used in making important educational decisions regarding, for example, the curriculum of educational institutions. Yet a view of indoctrination that is based exclusively on the intention of the teacher cannot exclude even the most pernicious doctrines from the curriculum. While no educational policy maker can control the intentions of teachers, every responsive educational planner can purify the curriculum by eliminating doctrinal beliefs from it.

The third objection to the intention criterion is that it overlooks the unintended consequences of human actions. Just as we can insult, embarrass, infuriate or intimidate other people without having the slightest intention of doing so, we can indoctrinate or otherwise miseducate them unintentionally. Educational and social planning that overlooks the unintended consequences of our actions, programmes, policies, institutional arrangements and so on must surely be considered narrow, unrealistic, reactionary and impoverished. It concentrates exclusively on the elusive intentions of teachers and overlooks the actual consequences of our interventions in the lives of the young.

Finally, the proponents of the intention criterion of indoctrination consistently overlook the fact that, like education, indoctrination also has a success or achievement sense. When we consider that aspect of indoctrination, intention becomes simply irrelevant. The only criterion that is relevant here is the specific doctrine(s) to which the novices are expected to commit themselves; if there is no commitment to such doctrine(s) we can no longer talk about indoctrination—regardless of the intentions of indoctrinators.

INDOCTRINATION AND METHODS

The last argument against the intention criterion also applies to the method criterion of indoctrination. The methods used by indoctrinators are irrelevant when we want to ascertain whether a person has been indoctrinated; commitment to certain doctrinal beliefs is the only relevant criterion.

In order for method to be an adequate criterion of indoctrination there must be methods peculiar to it. It is obvious, however, that there are no such methods. The indoctrinator, because he is inculcating doctrines, must resort to some educationally questionable methods such as failing to provide relevant evidence and arguments or misapplying them, misusing his authority and so on. These and other such methods, however, can be used for all sorts of educationally illegitimate purposes, not just indoctrination. An account of indoctrination in terms of method alone makes it synonymous with miseducation and thus renders it a useless, blunt tool. The issue is not whether indoctrination is miseducation but what sort of miseducation it is and how it differs from other sorts of miseducation; for example, the proponents of the method criterion invariably fail to distinguish between indoctrination and propaganda.[3] All theocratic and quasi-theocratic states resort to indoctrination in order to maintain or promote their status quo. Although propagandists often resort to indoctrination it is not necessary that they do so. In typical cases the indoctrinator believes that his doctrines are true or give meaning to life, or that they will bring about peace and justice on earth. In trying to inculcate his doctrines the indoctrinator offers some reasons and some evidence—it is another matter that his reasons and his evidence are based on sectarian, subjective grounds. Although at some point the indoctrinator will have to resort to non-rational methods, he does not have to behave like the pernicious propagandist who conceals or misrepresents facts, appeals to emotions or resorts to threats, hides his real motives and so on, in order to influence the beliefs and attitudes of people for the advancement of his own self-interest.

Indoctrination is a form of miseducation because it violates the knowledge criterion of education. But not every such violation could be properly called indoctrination; it is one thing, for example, to pass on doctrines which are in principle unfalsifiable beliefs, and it is another thing to pass on scientific theories *as if* they were doctrines. In the former case the doctrinal beliefs are in principle groundless; in the latter case the grounds for holding the beliefs have been omitted. There is absolutely no good reason to conflate these two cases of miseducation as if they were instances of the same kind of problem. The former could be described as a form of cosmic impiety whereas the latter is one of the many different kinds of miseducation. This is why the claim that indoctrination 'is aimed at developing a non-evidential way of holding beliefs' and therefore 'it is possible to indoctrinate people into truth' (Green, 1971, p. 50) is odd, indefensible and confusing; it obliterates an important distinction without any sound argument and without any support from ordinary language.

Furthermore, as we saw earlier, although propaganda and indoctrination are both forms of miseducation they are not the same kind of problem; and there are countless other forms of miseducation that must be distinguished from one another so that we can find the appropriate ways of dealing with them. If the teacher is teaching a scientific theory non-evidentially we can educate him so that he can teach it with the appropriate evidence and arguments. If, however, the teacher is passing on to his students unfalsifiable doctrinal beliefs we must help him to understand what he is doing so that he *stops* doing it. When teachers transmit to their students their own personal preferences, superstitions, prejudices and other non-evidentially held beliefs they are certainly miseducating but not necessarily indoctrinating. Those who conflate all these problems under the term indoctrination do not have a perspicuous view either of indoctrination or of these other problems.

Finally, the proponents of the method criterion of indoctrination assume that being rational is simply thinking in a certain manner. Yet as we shall see later, being rational is not just a matter of thinking and acting in a certain manner or form but also a matter of *thinking certain things*.

THE NATURE OF DOCTRINES

The most common reason given for abandoning doctrinal content as a necessary condition of indoctrination is that the term 'doctrine' is extremely vague (cf. Snook, 1972, p. 32). The problem with that claim is that even if true it would still be a *non sequitur*. If the word 'doctrine' were vague that would make 'indoctrination' a vague concept—it would not constitute a good reason for abandoning the criterion.

Very often this claim about vagueness is confused and the real problem is one of ambiguity, not vagueness. Words are used ambiguously when it is not clear from the context how they are supposed to be understood. The mere fact that words have variable meaning does not make them ambiguous. We talk, for example, of 'sharp criticism', 'sharp knives' and 'sharp students' without ever getting confused about the meaning of the word 'sharp' in these three contexts. Let us then adopt a similar approach while we look at the uses of the word 'doctrine' in its various contexts. The word 'doctrine' is sometimes used to mean 'theory' ('Einstein's doctrine of relativity'), 'principle' or 'policy' ('the Monroe doctrine') and rarely 'rule' ('the doctrine of do unto others. . .') or 'presupposition' ('the doctrine that every event has a cause'). In its plural form the word is used to refer to the teachings of wise persons ('The Doctrines of Great Educators'). To find out whether the word 'doctrine' is used in any of the above senses we must see if we can substitute any of them for the word 'doctrine'; if we cannot, then we can be fairly sure that what is being talked about is a real doctrine. The detection of real doctrines does not require special training and skills; only a very ignorant or retarded person would insist that the doctrine of the infallibility of the Pope or of the Second Coming is actually a theory. We now have a rule of thumb for distinguishing doctrines from non-doctrines, but we have not yet discussed the nature of doctrines and how they differ from non-doctrines.

The original and proper home of doctrines is religion, and the paradigm cases of indoctrination take place in theological schools or seminaries where the study of doctrines is one of their main subjects. In any other department of human enquiry doctrines are like dead rats in epistemological sanctuaries—when they are pointed out by critics they cause great embarrassment to their originators or perpetrators. And there is no canonical repentance available to scientists and others for their mistakes as there might be for religious 'heretics'. The talk about 'Marx's doctrines', 'Skinner's doctrines' or 'Freud's doctrines' might be intended as criticism of some of the most questionable ideas of these men—unless it is simply casual, unguarded talk. In such instances the onus is always on the speaker to demonstrate that some ideas of Marx, Skinner or Freud are indeed doctrines.[4] One must show, for example, that claims like 'Every historical event is the product of economic forces', 'Operant response increases in its probability when followed by a reinforcing situation' or 'All human actions are determined by unconscious forces' are unfalsifiable beliefs beyond any rational criticism—like religious doctrines.

There are two views about the nature of religious doctrines, which I would like to label: the literal *hard* view and the figurative *soft* view. According to the hard view (a) doctrines are in principle unfalsifiable beliefs about the existence of beings, states of affairs or relationships. Clear cases of doctrines are the belief in the triadic nature of the Christian deity and the belief in the infallibility of the Pope. (b) Doctrines are neither criteria of rationality nor irrationality; they are outside the rational tradition. That is why well-educated people may accept a doctrine and equally well-educated people may reject it. (c) Doctrines are not isolated beliefs but form a system of interrelated beliefs that constitutes the foundation of a particular world view, defines human nature, and determines man's 'proper' place in the world. This system of doctrines is an all-embracing, totalizing view that encompasses every aspect of human life as subsidiary. (d) There is a disparity between the linguistic form of a doctrine and its actual function within the system. Although all doctrines are descriptive statements (for example 'Jesus is the Son of God') they have an overriding prescriptive function within their respective contexts. For devout Catholics, for example, the doctrine of the infallibility of the Pope is not meant to be an idle belief—they are expected to obey the infallible Pope. Doctrines, then, are disguised, indirect prescriptions and their violations are not deemed to be normal human errors but punishable sins. (e) Finally, as the last point implies, doctrines presuppose the existence of authorities or institutions which have the power to uphold them when they are challenged by the critics, the heretics, or the faithless and to punish the enemies. Without an institution that articulates, orders and defends its doctrines they are in danger of deteriorating into common prejudices, or being abandoned.

Although all doctrines within a doctrinal system meet conditions (a), (b) and (e), not all such doctrines may meet conditions (c) and (d). The reason is that not all doctrines are of equal importance to the system at all times—some may be idle or dead remnants from earlier ways of life and are preserved merely as parts of a tradition.

With the exception of some epistemically primordial beliefs (which I shall discuss later), the only beliefs, outside religious doctrines, that are *clearly* unfalsifiable are common superstitions—a reason perhaps why some people consider all religious beliefs to be nothing more than superstitions. Superstitions, however, are usually isolated beliefs held by individuals and do not have the broad scope and the overriding prescriptive function of religious doctrines. Moreover, the charge of superstition depends on how one interprets doctrines; they resemble superstitions only if one interprets them to be literal claims, as many people do. But that is not the only way one can interpret doctrines. According to the second, soft view, doctrines, like other religious beliefs, are 'rules of life dressed up in pictures'. And these pictures only serve to describe what we are to do, not justify it. They could provide a justification only if they held good in other respects as well. Religion says: Do this!—Think like that!—but it cannot justify this and once it even tries to, it becomes repellent; because for every reason it offers there is a valid counter-reason (Wittgenstein, 1980, p. 29e).

Doctrinal beliefs according to this view are not ordinary knowledge claims that can be refuted nor are they hypotheses, opinions, views, conjectures that could be 'possibly', 'perhaps' or 'probably' confirmed or disconfirmed. Anything that we call scientific evidence is, according to Wittgenstein, irrelevant to this interpretation of religious belief. Even the most convincing forecast about the coming of the Day of Judgement would not influence a religious person because 'belief in this happening would not be at all a religious belief . . . the best scientific evidence is just nothing . . .' (Wittgenstein, 1967, p. 56). Although doctrinal beliefs appear to have a referent they are really about something else: 'The way you use the word "God" does not show whom you mean—but, rather, what you mean' (Wittgenstein, 1980, p. 50e); 'It strikes me', says Wittgenstein, 'that a religious belief could only be something like a passionate commitment to a system of reference. Hence, although it's belief, it's really a way of living, or a way of assessing life' (1980, p. 64e). 'Confusing religious doctrines with empirical ones is a blunder that reduces all such beliefs to superstition.' Wittgenstein repeatedly argued that religious belief 'not only is . . . not reasonable, but . . . doesn't pretend to be', and that it is 'ludicrous' to make it 'appear to be reasonable' (1967, p. 58). About those who try to make religious belief appear to be reasonable by appealing to facts and evidence, Wittgenstein says that they are unreasonable and that 'if this is religious belief, it's all superstition' (1967, p. 59).

The distinction between the hard and the soft views of doctrines sketched here is rarely made by religious believers; they usually equivocate by sliding from one into the other. I think it would be reasonable to claim that if we accept the above analysis of doctrines, most of what passes as religion today is superstition. What is of educational interest in this analysis is that however one interprets doctrines they do not belong within our rational tradition and therefore they should have no place in our educational institutions. Under the first description they are largely superstitions, whereas under the second they are personal perspectives on the world and on human life—and therefore subjective preferences. It is not being argued here, of course, that we should not teach the young *about* the various religions, the various perspectives they provide on life, their histories and their influences on various cultures. It is argued that we have no educational justification for indoctrinating people into the doctrines of a particular religion.

DOCTRINES AND THE FOUNDATIONS OF RATIONALITY

It has been argued by several writers that indoctrination is unavoidable in education because it is a prerequisite to the introduction of the young into our rational heritage, including science. 'The basic assumptions and postulates of an empirical science,' says Snook, 'qualify as doctrines' (1972, p. 35). Likewise, Thomas Green maintains that 'Indoctrination . . . has a perfectly good and important role to play in education . . . Indoctrination may be necessary as a prelude to teaching' (1972, pp. 44–5). Content, then, according to these writers, cannot be a criterion of indoctrination since the presuppositions of our rational discourse are equally non-rational. But is this all that can be said about the nature of doctrines and the foundations of our rational modes of thinking?

In the remainder of this chapter I want to show that there is a world of difference between doctrines, as I described them earlier, and what Wittgenstein, in *On Certainty* (1969), called the 'river-bed' (par. 97), the 'axis' (par. 152) , the 'scaffolding' (par. 211), the 'hinges' (par. 341) and the 'unmoving foundations' (par. 403) of all our thoughts, judgements, language and actions. In fact, when I have enumerated the important differences it should become obvious that the similarities between them are superficial and trivial.

It is never made clear by the above writers what they mean by 'assumptions', 'presuppositions', 'postulates' or 'fundamentals' of science. We can identify, however, a great number of propositions that belong to the bedrock of all our thinking and therefore of science which are not doctrines. Wittgenstein says: 'Propositions of the form of empirical propositions, and not only propositions of logic, form the foundation of all operating with thoughts (language)' (1969, par. 401) Among these propositions we can distinguish some that are pseudo-empirical because they are in fact methodological propositions, that is, rules that are presupposed by any language games we may engage in. They are not propositions that can be doubted, tested, confirmed, or about which one can be mistaken. Examples of such propositions are: 'Physical objects exist' and 'Objects continue in existence when not perceived'. Any attempt to deny such propositions leads to absurdity.

There are, next, empirical propositions about which we 'can hardly be mistaken' (1969, par. 673). Examples of such propositions are: 'I have two hands', 'I am a human being', 'Automobiles do not grow on trees' and the like. Reasonable people have plenty of doubts, says Wittgenstein, but not about these and a great number of similar propositions. Only 'insane', 'mad', 'demented', or 'idiotic' people would express doubt about such propositions and their doubt would be 'hollow', 'senseless' and 'without consequence' (1969, par. 468, 281, 155, 662, 257, 312, 56, 310, 338). These and similar river-bed propositions, then, together with propositions of logic and methodological propositions, constitute criteria of rationality about which one cannot be mistaken. A person who insists that his head is stuffed with straw is not making a mistake, he is mentally disturbed. 'Being reasonable', says Thomas Morawetz, 'is not just a matter of acting and thinking in a certain manner or form but also a matter of thinking certain things' (1987, p. 75).

Now that we have sketched the nature of doctrines and the nature of the river-bed propositions that lie at the foundations of all our thinking, we can see more clearly the radical differences between them. First, belief or disbelief in doctrines is not a criterion of rationality, whereas doubting or questioning of river-bed propositions is a sign of organic mental disturbance. I cannot make a mistake about the fact that I am a human being or that I am right now in Canada.

Secondly, there are alternatives to particular doctrines but not to the river-bed certainties. One can doubt, question, accept, modify or abandon doctrinal beliefs but not river-bed propositions. Catholics believe in the *filioque* whereas Greek Orthodox Christians deny it; neither, however, can deny that physical objects exist.

Thirdly, river-bed propositions are *acquired* or inherited without any thinking, investigation or justification. These ordinary certainties are not matter of knowledge and must be taught as a foundation, substratum or background without evidence and without reasons. 'Knowing only begins at a later level', says Wittgenstein (1969, par. 358), when there is 'a possibility of demonstrating the truth' (ibid., par. 243). Doctrines, on the other hand, are learned. There is nothing in human experience that requires the doctrine of the infallibility of the Pope or of the *filioque*, whereas everything in human experience presupposes the law of induction or the existence of physical objects.

Fourthly, whereas all explanations and justifications come to an end, that end is not doctrines that can be doubted but the river-bed propositions, which cannot. Since river-bed propositions are the foundations of all our thought, language and action, they must also be the foundations of all our talk about doctrines. It follows, therefore, that doctrines are not at the same epistemic level as river-bed certainties. So the onus is on the proponents of indoctrination to show where doctrines belong since they are not knowledge claims either.

Finally, a word about the functions of the river-bed propositions and of doctrines. While the former enable us to think, the latter act as *stoppers* that control, limit and channel free thought, disallow alternative beliefs, and frustrate critical thinking. That is the reason why indoctrination is inherently authoritarian: it claims that there are no alternatives whereas, in fact, there are many; it aims at legitimating political authority and power, silencing the opponents and controlling people's lives. The recent actions of the Vatican to uphold and expand the doctrinal beliefs of the Catholic church are good examples of what I am talking about.

DOCTRINES AND FREEDOM

As must be obvious from the above, indoctrination has profound consequences for the way of thinking and acting of the individual citizen as well as for the nature of the social order. At the individual level indoctrination may control and channel people's thinking to such an extent that they come to abhor alternative ways of thinking and behaving. The inculcated doctrines are not isolated beliefs that may be altered by arguments and evidence; they provide a comprehensive picture of the world that pervades people's thinking, orders their lives and renders them incapable of entertaining the possibility of changing their beliefs and ways of life. In talking about the effect of making people think in accordance with doctrines Ludwig Wittgenstein makes the following pertinent observations.

> I am not thinking of these dogmas as determining men's opinions but rather as completely controlling the *expression* of all opinions. People will live under an absolute, palpable tyranny, though without being able to say they are not free. I think the Catholic Church does something rather like this. For dogma is expressed in the form of an assertion, and it is unshakeable. . . . It is not a wall setting limits to what can be believed, but more like a brake which, however practically serves the same purpose; it's almost as though someone were to attach a weight to your foot to restrict your freedom of movement. This is how dogma becomes irrefutable and beyond the reach of attack (1980, p. 28e).

An extraordinary example of this kind of problem is Isaac Newton's unwillingness or inability to change his views about 'absolute position, or absolute space, as it was called, because it did not accord with his idea of an absolute God. In fact, he refused to accept lack of absolute space, even though it was implied by his laws. He was severely criticized for this irrational belief by many people, most notably by Bishop Berkeley' (Hawking, 1988, p. 18).

It must be this foundational position of doctrines in determining a person's way of life that makes them so difficult to dislodge or, as Wittgenstein says, 'irrefutable and beyond the reach of attack'. This is the reason why indoctrinators are most interested and effective in inculcating their doctrines in young children, whereas propagandists direct their propaganda more widely. Although the propagandist is sinister, he still knows that evidence and reasons are powerful in altering people's beliefs and commitments; that is the reason why propaganda is fought with counter-propaganda. Unlike the indoctrinator, the propagandist does not abandon evidence and arguments, he perverts them. The indoctrinator, on the other hand, knows that if he is successful in instilling his unfalsifiable doctrines in the minds of the young they will become immunized against reason and arguments.

Recent developments in Eastern Europe confirm these points about indoctrination and propaganda. What held the communist regimes in power in these countries was not the political quasi-indoctrination but mainly propaganda backed by force; that is why there was the possibility for change, and they are now changing. The Catholic church, on the other hand, has lasted and will last for many more centuries because it is founded on doctrines and has one of the most sophisticated programmes of indoctrination.

As I mentioned at the beginning of this chapter, one of the reasons we are concerned about indoctrination is that it has serious consequences for the social order. While indoctrinated people are unable or unwilling to see the subjective nature of their parochial doctrines, they still want their doctrinal beliefs to function as regulative principles of the way of life of the whole community. Their view of the good life and the code of conduct that is embedded in their world view are parasitic on their doctrinal framework, which cannot withstand public scrutiny on the basis of intersubjective criteria and canons of sound reasoning.

By 'completely controlling the *expression* of all opinions', as Wittgenstein said, indoctrination delimits the scope of human thought and action, discourages alternative views and thus impoverishes human life and culture. It is the most pernicious form of authoritarianism and is practised in all closed societies.

NOTES

(1) An earlier version of this chapter entitled 'Indoctrination, doctrines and the foundations of rationality', appeared in *Philosophy of Education 1987: Proceedings of the Forty-third Annual Meeting of the Philosophy of Education Society*. Normal, Illinois: Philosophy of Education Society, 1987.

(2) Even the notorious Trofim Lysenko, who tried to revive Lamarckian views of heredity in the Soviet Union with the help of Stalin and the Central Committee of the Communist Party, was not promoting a doctrine but a defunct theory that happened to agree with the prevailing political ideology in that country—his views were not, in principle, unfalsifiable.

(3) Harvey Siegel, for example, in his book *Educating Reason* (1988, p. 81) asks: 'Is it the case . . . that education necessarily involves "propaganda"? Is indoctrination inevitable?', thus implying that the two terms are synonymous.

(4) For a recent discussion of the alleged tautologies/doctrines contained in Darwin's Theory see Sober (1984) Ch. 2.

REFERENCES

Austin, J. L. (1961) *Philosophical Papers*. London: Oxford University Press.

Green, T. F. (1971) *The Activities of Teaching*. New York: McGraw-Hill.

Green, T. F. (1972) Indoctrination and beliefs. In I. A. Snook (ed.) *Concepts of Indoctrination*. London: Routledge & Kegan Paul.

Hawking, S. W. (1988) *A Brief History of Time*. Toronto: Bantam Books.

Morawetz, T. (1987) *Wittgenstein and Knowledge*. Atlantic Highlands, NJ: Humanities Press.

Siegel, H. (1988) *Educating Reason: Rationality, Critical Thinking, and Education*. London: Routledge & Kegan Paul.

Snook, I. A. (ed.) (1972) *Indoctrination and Education*. London: Routledge & Kegan Paul.

Sober, E. (1984) *The Nature of Selection: Evolutionary Theory in Philosophical Focus*. Cambridge, MA: MIT Press.

Strawson, P. F. (1963) *Individuals*. New York: Doubleday.

Wittgenstein, L. (1967) *Lectures and Conversations on Aesthetics, Psychology and Religious Belief*. Berkeley, CA: University of California Press.

Wittgenstein, L. (1969) *On Certainty*. New York: Harper & Row.

Wittgenstein, L. (1980) *Culture and Value*. Oxford: Basil Blackwell.

Chapter 2

Indoctrination: The Suppression of Critical Dispositions[1]

Ben Spiecker

INTRODUCTION

There is hardly a consensus on how to use the term 'indoctrination' (see Snook, 1972). Much remains to be clarified about the content criterion of 'indoctrination', particularly the meaning of 'doctrine'. Looking back at the developments of ten years in the field of philosophy of education, R. S. Peters observed that the controversy over 'indoctrination' would have been considerably clarified if what constitutes a 'doctrine' had been more decisively determined (1983, p. 46).

In this chapter I will try to demonstrate that Peters was right, and argue that a further analysis of 'inculcating doctrines' will show this term to be a sufficient condition for the correct use of 'indoctrination'. Inculcating doctrines is always associated with the suppression of a critical attitude. Indoctrination can also be understood as the suppression of a critical attitude, as the hampering of intellectual virtues and rational emotions. This analysis will be compared with other interpretations of indoctrination, especially with Kohlberg's view of indoctrination and moral education. Finally, the issue will be raised whether only children or juveniles can be the victims of indoctrination. Can critical thinkers or (morally) educated people also be subjected to indoctrination? It is argued that in these cases it makes more sense to use the term 'brainwashing'.

DOCTRINES AND INDOCTRINATION

What makes a belief, or a set of beliefs, a doctrine? As a result of Popperian and post-Popperian developments in the philosophy of science we no longer have to answer this question with notions like 'publicly accepted evidence' and 'empirical testability'. Doctrines, as a special class of beliefs, relate to issues that are considered to be of the utmost importance to us, like the nature and ultimate destination of mankind and the way in which a just society is to be organized. A (system of) doctrine(s) is no pure academic or theoretical matter; its adherents feel obliged to conform to strict rules of behaviour and to commit themselves to specific ideas. Marxism-Leninism, according to Gregory and Woods, dictates what its followers shall do: how they are to educate their children, what to teach their students, what sorts of works artists have to produce, how industry and the social institutions are to be organized (1972, p. 166). A second condition of 'doctrines'—one that, in my opinion, has hitherto been somewhat neglected in the discussions—is that this class of beliefs or propositions is screened, by the people who subscribe to them, from criticism, from questions about their *validity*, be it empirical, normative or conceptual. Doctrines also persist by virtue of non-critical attitudes. It is this second condition that normally prevents us from speaking about 'indoctrination of students in science and mathematics'. Let me illustrate the above with an example. A journalist concludes, after a visit to the communist Republic of Albania in 1985, that daily life in that country is a product of a successful *'total indoctrination'*. The Albanians use no 'double talk' and they defend with a moving honesty the horrors they have to endure in the name of the Party. They are 'cured' of thinking; the state thinks for them. The state decides where one lives, where and how hard one works, where and what one studies, where one is allowed to go, what one reads and hears, the amount of money one earns and what to buy with it, when one has a vacation and where to spend it, where and when one has to do 'voluntary' work. But these people live in a safe and protected world. Nothing can happen to them as long as they walk in step; they have a guaranteed income and no hard decisions to make. Their world is full of certainties, and the 'outer' world does not interest them—that is the world where the Mafia and capitalism reign (Michielsen, 1985). Here the doctrinal statements of the Party have the status of non-falsifiable or revealed truths; dissidents or renegades are not so much in 'error' as 'morally' reprehensible: they have committed a 'mortal sin'.

I can now summarize the two necessary conditions for the correct use of 'doctrines', which together are sufficient: (1) doctrines are those systems of belief that to a large extent determine the doings and dealings of the adherents, and (2) doctrines are those beliefs that are screened from criticism, from a critical attitude. There is a close connection between the second condition of 'doctrines' and the linguistic fact that we talk about 'inculcating doctrines'. For 'inculcating' connotes the suppression of a certain critical attitude. Indoctrination can also be understood as the inculcation of doctrines. The successfully indoctrinated person is necessarily doctrinaire (person who applies principle without allowance for circumstances, *Concise Oxford Dictionary*). But does this also apply to the indoctrinator? I do not think so; a person who himself is averse to doctrines can very well be a skilled indoctrinator.

The inculcation of doctrines can never happen by accident; to indoctrinate is to suppress wilfully (the development of) the critical disposition of the students. This can be done by a gamut of non-rational methods: by an appeal to an Absolute Authority, by violating the canons of reasoning, by smuggling away relevant evidence, by ignoring critical questions and by conjuring up feelings of guilt and anxiety (cf. Kazepides, 1974).

The thesis that the (moral) indoctrinator pursues the suppression or the breaking down of the critical disposition has also been defended by R. M. Hare (1972). The indoctrinator, according to Hare, tries to make his pupils perpetual children; so indoctrination begins when we try to stop the growth in our children of the capacity to think for themselves about (moral) questions (1972, p. 52).

With reference to what has already been said about doctrines, I can now conclude that indoctrination is connected to that class of beliefs that stimulates the suppression of the disposition for critical reflection. Doctrines that to a large extent permeate the individual's existence, that completely define the meaning of life, suffering and death, are most suited to making a person doctrinaire and incapable of reflecting critically. This, incidentally, does not mean that beliefs or certainties that form the 'heart of our existence' cannot also serve pre-eminently to sharpen our critical dispositions.

INTELLECTUAL VIRTUES AND RATIONAL EMOTIONS

'Indoctrination' has a pejorative meaning because in the process one's fellow-man is approached in a morally unacceptable manner. In his pedagogical activities the sincere educator must be committed not only to certain values like honesty, conscientiousness and integrity, but also to moral principles like having respect for persons and considering the interests of other people. In the process of influencing others the indoctrinator not only sets aside these values and principles, but also intends, with regard to the doctrines to be indoctrinated, to prevent his pupils from acquiring the character traits or virtues that correspond to these principles. Here the addition 'with regard to . . .' is of importance, because the same teacher-indoctrinator can very well pursue the development of a critical disposition in other domains of knowledge and experience. In the USSR, according to Peters, people are discouraged from questioning the validity of their moral and political beliefs but, on the other hand, are encouraged to deploy their critical capacities in the domains of technology and mathematics, and in chess (1974, p. 349).

To indoctrinate is 'to still critical reflection' or 'to stimulate being doctrinaire' with regard to certain beliefs and can be characterized as the systematic suppression of specific traits of character or virtues in relation to certain beliefs. To be more specific, the suppression of the intellectual virtues and rational emotions is particularly at stake here. To protect the indisputable and indubitable character of certain beliefs, the indoctrinator forces his pupils to acquire intellectual *vices* and *ir*rational emotions.

Intellectual virtues are dispositions that we practise when we examine (that is, when we *think* about) the validity of arguments and beliefs. Demands for evidence, the search for grounds for beliefs, impartiality, consistency, being unprejudiced, cautiousness, and the courage to reconsider one's opinion are dispositions that are constitutive of every developed use of reason. The bearer of these intellectual virtues will practise these traits of character in the way she thinks. Her thinking is characterized by the virtues of open-mindedness and intellectual fairness; she examines the strength of counter-arguments, is alert to her own possible prejudices, can admit her own fallacies and does justice to the arguments of others.

Intellectual virtues correspond with different types of procedural rules, especially with constitutive procedural rules that determine the *relevance* of arguments and with regulative procedural rules that determine effective ways of finding out the *truth* of those arguments. The first type of rules forms the 'logic' of a specific form of thinking (scientific, moral), the second type bears on all forms of thinking. To be able and willing to reflect critically on a moral dilemma, for instance, a person must have acquired both types of procedural rules; she must be able and willing to follow both the constitutive rule of impartiality (or formal justice) in her moral thinking, and the regulative rules regarding intellectual modesty and thoroughness. Regulative intellectual virtues imply a willingness to learn from criticism, to refrain from intellectual arrogance and to found moral judgements on solid arguments; these virtues correspond to regulative rules which have the typical function of maximizing the chance of having true or justified moral beliefs (cf. Steutel, 1989).

To indoctrinate a person is not only to try to suppress her intellectual virtues, it is also aimed at impeding the development of her rational emotions. Rational emotions form an integral part of our cognitive functioning: love of veracity or truth and integrity, contempt for lying, abhorrence of unclarity and inaccuracy. After all, teachers want their students to *value* and to *love* good reasoning, to *care* about reason and its use (cf. Siegel, 1988, pp. 39, 40).

According to Scheffler, surprise or astonishment can also be called a rational emotion; the testing and revising of theories call upon such emotional dispositions. A dogmatic or doctrinaire person not only avoids the systematic testing of his beliefs, he denies also, from the outset, the existence of negative evidence. According to Scheffler, he blocks surprise not by disclaiming responsibility for his doctrines, but by denying the experience that contradicts them. The observations of this person are theory-laden to the point of blindness, and the joy he takes in verification is thus unearned and hollow (1977, p. 184).

In this context Siegel makes an important psychological observation. The critical thinker has a rich emotional make-up of dispositions, habits of mind, values, character traits and emotions, but besides having these qualities, the critical thinker must be, to the greatest extent possible, emotionally secure and self-confident. A positive self-image and psychological 'health' are important features of the *psychology* of the critical thinker; absence of these qualities may well constitute an obstacle to the execution of critical thinking (Siegel, 1988, p. 41).

The intellectual vices and irrational emotions, like unreliability, contempt for the facts and irrational feelings of anxiety and guilt, which form the counterpart of the intellectual virtues and rational emotions, will impede the indoctrinated person from bringing his beliefs up for discussion. That is why, as Green rightly observes, the indoctrinated person will tend to use argument, evidence and criticism not as an instrument of enquiry, but as an instrument to establish what he already believes (1971, p. 50). What Popper (1982) calls the *petty-minded* evil also falls under the intellectual vices: arrogance, self-conceit, intellectual vanity and pedantry. The doctrinaire or dogmatic person cannot help but cling to his own rightness in a spasmodic and obstinate, that is an irrational, way. So if Peters describes moral indoctrination as 'a process that drastically discourages the fundamental questioning of the validity of rules which characterises the autonomous stage' (1974, p. 356), we now better understand which intellectual vices and irrational feelings hamper the person in question from functioning at the level of moral autonomy. These same vices and feelings explain why the aim of indoctrination can also be understood as 'developing a nonevidential way of holding beliefs' (cf. Green, 1971, p. 50).

Let me illustrate this analysis with an example. In an interview the Dutch Roman Catholic cardinal A. J. Simonis states:

Some with all their criticism think that in the church something like 'loyal opposition' is possible. Now, if bishops did behave in an obscene way—I do not know any one who does—yes, then opposition certainly would be necessary, but opposition against the doctrines of the church and her sexual morality, that are said to be backward, this is inadmissible, this is not loyal, because it goes against the authentic Christian doctrine. (*NRC/Handelsblad*, 10 May 1985)

The cardinal explicitly appeals to feelings of guilt in the believers, by referring to lack of loyalty and trust. He is also of the opinion that protests against the papal nomination of bishops in the Netherlands are unjustifiable 'for the decisions over these nominations are always taken with great wisdom and after much prayer'. So for the cardinal practising the intellectual virtues in this matter is nothing less than expressing distrust in the dialogue between the head of the Roman Catholic church and God. How is the doubter to react to the thought of his mistaken distrust other than by having feelings of guilt, shame and anxiety? Especially in relation to religious indoctrination the role of irrational feelings is not to be underestimated. By appealing to the possible loss of the eternal salvation of one's soul, the preacher-indoctrinator can arouse tremendous irrational fear in both child and adult.

The central conditions of 'indoctrination', as we have seen, are *content* (doctrines) and *intention* (to still the development of a critical attitude with regard to certain beliefs). There is a logical connection between the two conditions: in order for doctrines to stay well beyond all doubt, the intellectual virtues and rational emotions are to be suppressed; and the acquisition of intellectual vices and irrational feelings is promoted by the inculcation of doctrinaire beliefs. Doctrines are those beliefs that have the potential to promote the aforementioned vices and feelings. In particular those beliefs which refer to the meaning of life, the (ultimate or eternal) destiny and origin of mankind and the final goal of history have enormous potential to arouse feelings of fear, guilt, despair and zealotry. It is hard to imagine how (often incomprehensible) formulae from nuclear physics or astronomy, which do not directly relate to the question of the meaning of our lives, can possibly give rise to such irrational feelings. Thinking about human evolution, on the other hand, is all too often obscured by anthropocentric emotions and religious beliefs, because it touches on questions about the ultimate meaning of human existence. The tenacious defence of the so-called 'science' of creationism can serve as an illustration.

To indoctrinate a person is to be understood as inducing a stunted development in one or more domains of knowledge and experience. But the formation of the critical dispositions is not tied to one specific domain, and here the indoctrinator is confronted with a problem as large as life; if he wants to suppress a critical attitude in the 'indoctrination-prone' domains of religion, politics and morality he will have to see to it that his students do not transfer to these domains the dispositions they have acquired during their instruction and training in mathematics and science. To ban these domains altogether ('Cultural Revolution') may be thought too high a price to pay.

The idea that 'indoctrination' is connected with 'doctrines' and 'intention' is not shared by other philosophers. In order to test my analysis I will explore to what extent I can meet their arguments. Thereafter I shall demonstrate that the analysis of 'indoctrination' is of the utmost importance for our understanding of the moral education and development of children.

INDOCTRINATION, DOCTRINE AND INTENTION

An argument against the logical connection between 'doctrines' and 'indoctrination' is that, given the fact that doctrines are held in an incorrigible manner, then science, too, contains many doctrines, yet we do not indoctrinate students in science (cf. Thiessen, 1984, p. 32). This argument, however, cuts no ice, for the sciences (even the social sciences)—though no doubt they do contain doctrines—are constituted in principle by the rule that all propositions are to be tested on their validity. The mere fact that the first-order principles or presuppositions of science are non-falsifiable does not, as Thiessen believes, make them doctrines. The postulate of causality is of a transcendental character, but is never excluded from discussion (quantum theory), but we rightly speak of the doctrine of the Immaculate Conception, because discussion of the validity (empirical?, conceptual?) of this proposition is ruled out (*ex cathedra*).

The connection between 'doctrine' and the suppression of intellectual virtues and rational emotions implies that doctrines need not be conceived as propositions 'not known to be true or false', or as propositions that are 'unverifiable and unfalsifiable' (cf. White, 1972, p. 193). White defends the weaker claim that 'indoctrination' need not involve actual doctrines using as an example a schoolteacher in a working-class district who tries to stamp into his pupils the belief that they are fitted only to become manual workers. He does so not by getting the pupils to accept any system of beliefs, but by taking them on visits to factories and so on 'designed to make them feel that manual work is for them' (1972, p. 194). According to White, an opponent of his (weaker) claim will not accept this as an example of indoctrination since it involves no doctrine. In my terms, however, a doctrinal belief is at issue in this example: the belief that is stamped into the pupils can (and ought to) be tested on its normative validity. Moreover, the feelings (or better, emotions) of these pupils do have a cognitive component, which can also be subjected to critical appraisal. So when White argues against his imaginary opponent that his example is a case of indoctrination, because the teacher 'is trying to implant a belief of some sort or another in such a way that this is never questioned' (p. 194), I fully agree with him for the very reason that the suppression of intellectual virtues and rational emotions relating to a belief is at issue.

Indoctrinative suppression of the critical dispositions can never happen by accident: it will always be pursued intentionally. The politician or curriculum planner can set the stage for indoctrination; but their intentions can effectively be realized only by educators willingly working within the framework of the curriculum. Referring to such a case, White states that they (the teachers) 'are not indoctrinators, I half wish to say, but rather unwitting tools in the real indoctrinators' hands. For each teacher there is nothing necessarily indoctrinatory about his work' (p. 198). According to my analysis, however, these teachers and educators can be blamed for stimulating the development of intellectual vices and irrational feelings in relation to the doctrine. After all, even when he is working from doctrinaire books, it is possible for a sincere and skilled teacher to sharpen the critical dispositions of his pupils. In face-to-face situations with his students almost nothing—no curriculum—and nobody—no politician—can stop an educated person from stimulating the critical attitude of children.

The thesis that we could indoctrinate *un*intentionally has also been defended by R. Beehler (1985). In his imaginary example a young man unintentionally gives an incorrect account of the history of the Indians to young children. This teacher, however, is conscious of his responsibility to develop the pupils' capacity to think and to judge for themselves, and he constantly invites and encourages questions and objections (p. 264). In short: he intentionally tries to promote their critical disposition. Now the question is: are these pupils being indoctrinated? According to Beehler, the truth or falsehood of what is 'taught' is irrelevant to this question. Even if what the teacher had presented to them were the truth, the children would still have been indoctrinated, for these young children lack both the psychological understanding of our passions (love and hate), and the historical understanding which would enable them to appraise intelligently the information: 'It is that what he is doing these children are not able to enter into' (p. 267). The response of these children can therefore only be: to accept and to believe. The teacher cannot help but indoctrinate.

Beehler apparently neglects the conceptual differences between 'indoctrination', 'initiation into forms of life', 'training' and 'socialization'. By calling 'doing something into which children cannot (yet) enter' indoctrination, he ignores the point that 'indoctrination' in general has a pejorative meaning. The teacher in his example is displaying his intellectual virtues and rational emotions and by setting the example of how to conduct a critical enquiry, he shows his pupils what counts as a critical attitude, and in this way he starts to train them in asking questions and making objections. By approaching his students in a *contra-factual* manner, *as if* they had already acquired intellectual virtues and rational emotions, this teacher helps to promote the development of these dispositions (see Spiecker, 1984). The teacher in Beehler's example is therefore a 'pedagogue *par excellence*', because he stimulates critical dispositions and also tries to avoid indoctrinating his pupils. For normal young pupils do have the potential to develop a critical attitude; if this human potential is missing, it hardly makes sense to use the term 'indoctrination'. ('He has tried to indoctrinate his severely mentally handicapped son.')

KOHLBERG AND MORAL INDOCTRINATION

Misunderstanding of 'indoctrination' can lead to an inadequate conception of certain aspects of moral education and development. This can be demonstrated in the studies of Kohlberg. In the 1970s Kohlberg was confronted with the dilemma of value inculcation versus value clarification in moral education. Does a teacher have the right to impose his values on the pupils or is he only allowed to help them to become aware of their own values? In the former case one could speak about the indoctrination of pupils. In the latter case it is implicitly presupposed that all values are relative, and it cannot be excluded in advance that the pupil will subscribe to racist or fascist beliefs and values.

Kohlberg finds the solution of this dilemma in his empirical cross-cultural findings, which show that the development of moral judgement takes place according to universal and invariant stages and that there are universal values (principles). The invariant sequence of moral judgements, according to Kohlberg, is not dependent on a specific ideology: 'I found no important differences in the development of moral thinking among Catholics, Protestants, Jews, Buddhists, Moslems, and atheists' (1971; in Kohlberg, 1981, p. 25). This insight enables educators to stimulate moral development without thereby making themselves guilty of indoctrination. The wish of progressive educators to educate their children to endorse the principles they themselves hold no longer need be characterized as indoctrination. It is this point that Kohlberg in his early studies presents as one of the justifications for the superiority (including *moral* superiority) of his developmental-philosophic approach, compared to what he then called the 'cultural bag' or 'desirable trait' and the 'cultural transmission' approaches (1972, p. 476). Educators only have to stimulate the 'natural' moral development of children into the next stage. In the words of Kohlberg:

> We have claimed that the experiences by which children naturally move from stage to stage are nonindoctrinative, that is, they are not experiences of being taught and internalizing specific content. These experiences are listed as those involving moral conflict (in the cognitive-conflict sense) and exposure to, higher modes of thinking than one's own. Insofar as the teacher deliberately uses such experiences as her method of moral education, she is not being 'indoctrinative'.
> (1980, p. 74)

The legitimacy of his developmental approach to moral education is also demonstrated by Kohlberg's claim that 'the stimulation of moral development defines an educational process respecting the autonomy of the child, whereas any other definition reflects indoctrination' (1980, p. 74). Having respect for the child's autonomy is a more legitimate concern than showing respect for the parent's or teacher's rights to transmit (to indoctrinate) their own values.

Kohlberg's anti-indoctrination argument, his views on the free choice of the child and on respect for his rights, can be seen as part of the 'protective belt' of his research programme. Still, it is surprising that this researcher has not based his anti-indoctrination argument, in which the teaching of moral content or the transmission of values is *ipso facto* indoctrination, on a more adequate elucidation of this central term. After all, Kohlberg himself has stressed the importance of the analysis of ordinary language: 'we justify our choice of studying the use of ordinary moral language . . . because we believe that if one leaves ordinary language behind one robs oneself of valuable empirical data' (Kohlberg *et al.*, 1983, p. 71; see also pp. 67, 70, 74). Contrary to 'indoctrination', 'transmission' (of moral content) does not necessarily have a pejorative meaning. Young children have the right to be taught (moral) rules and values. The term 'indoctrination' is only justified in those cases where rules and values are transmitted in such a manner that they acquire the character of doctrines.

It is no surprise that, because of his misinterpretation of this term, Kohlberg had to revise his view on the relation between moral education and indoctrination in his later studies. He then realized that the abstraction of moral content from moral judgement only served certain research purposes, and that these abstractions were not 'a sufficient guide to the moral educator who deals with the moral concrete in a school world in which value content as well as structure, behavior as well as reasoning, must be dealt with' (1978, p. 14). In a world where people, and thus also children, steal, deceive and treat fellow-citizens in an aggressive way we cannot wait till the children have reached the fifth stage of moral development before we start concentrating on their moral conduct. Teachers he has consulted—he also explicitly mentions the philosopher of education, Richard Peters—have convinced Kohlberg that moral education has to deal with content as well as with moral structure, and that the traditional 'character education' or 'teaching of virtues' is justified. He has then accepted the idea that the teacher is and should be an advocate of specific moral content: 'I now believe that moral education can be in the form of advocacy or 'indoctrination' without violating the child's rights, as long as teacher advocacy is democratic . . ., recognizing the shared rights of teachers and students' (1978, p. 85; 1985, p. 81).

In one of his last studies Kohlberg chooses a slightly different formulation: 'For me the thing that prevents teachers' advocacy from being indoctrination is the establishment of participatory democracy in the classroom or in the school' (1985, p. 82).

This reconstruction of the shift in Kohlberg's thinking about indoctrination shows how important it is in research on moral education and development to have an adequate conception of 'indoctrination'. This term has played a vital role in Kohlberg's theory construction. His first conception of it has played tricks on him in understanding the nature of moral education; his latest formulations, however, correspond to a large extent with the analysis of 'indoctrination' as the suppression of intellectual virtues and rational emotions, for to establish 'participatory democracy' in schools precisely implies the fostering and the execution of critical dispositions, of intellectual virtues and rational emotions.

The term 'moral indoctrination' refers to the inculcation of moral rules and prescriptions in such a manner that these rules acquire the character of doctrines. In the moral indoctrination of the child the question of the normative validity of social rules, conventions and prescriptions is systematically evaded. In other words, practising the rational emotions and intellectual virtues with respect to moral rules and conventions is systematically suppressed. Often these rules are presented as 'laws' dictated by an authority. So Dutch Calvinists during the Second World War struggled with the (moral) question of whether they were allowed to lie to German *Wehrmacht* soldiers, when they were asked by these oppressors whether they were hiding Jews. After all it is said in Romans 13:1 that everybody should obey state authorities, because no authority exists without God's permission, and because the existing authorities have been put there by God. Helping Jews go into hiding and to escape death could therefore be interpreted as acting against God's will (Romans 13:2: 'Whoever opposes the existing authority opposes what God has ordered; and anyone who does so will bring judgment on himself'). This ('moral') dilemma both gave rise to, and was fuelled by an intense (irrational) emotion, the fear of God's wrath. Unable to make a morally autonomous decision, a delegation of the Calvinists even went to Switzerland in order to consult Karl Barth, an authoritative theologian, on this issue.

TWO FORMS OF INDOCTRINATION?

'Indoctrination' is, as we have seen, connected with '*development*', and it is not by chance that many of the examples given refer to efforts to influence children or students, that is, those whose critical attitude has not yet fully developed. Indoctrination can be seen as a species of education, as a form of *mis*education because it is meant to prevent the child from becoming a certain sort of *person*, namely a critical thinker (cf. Siegel, 1988, p. 41). The indoctrinator in his relation to the pupil transgresses the moral rule of 'respect for persons'; he also prevents the child from becoming a moral person who is able to reflect on the validity of prevailing moral rules. In this way the middle-class rules or relative moral rules (Peters) acquire the status of rigid moral doctrines.

The consequence of this conception of indoctrination is that only those who have not yet acquired the critical dispositions can be the subjects of this form of influence. This view seems to contradict the fact that, according to reports in the past and in the present, people who have reached the years of discretion have fallen victim to indoctrination. Stalinists, Trotskyists, Methodists, Fascists, Catholics (Jesuits) and Calvinists have all used techniques of political and religious indoctrination in the battle for the minds of *adults* (see Sargant, 1957). In studies on religious conversion and political indoctrination, the authors often use 'indoctrination' of adults as synonymous with 'brainwashing'. I will try to show that this term 'indoctrination' has a different meaning in these contexts, that it has to do with systematic attempts to *destroy* the present critical dispositions in order to take possession of the 'emptied' mind. To illustrate my point I will make use of reports on the 'Chinese indoctrination programme', without ignoring the fact that these techniques have also been developed and successfully applied in our Western civilizations (the Inquisition and mass conversions).

Information on the Chinese indoctrination programme(s) stems from reports of the thought reform programmes after the Communist takeover in 1948–9 and of the programme for prisoners of war during the Korean war (cf. Lifton, 1962; Schein, 1956). The term 'thought *reform*' indicates precisely how indoctrination is to be understood in this context. The central question of the thought reformers is: how can a man be made to *change* his beliefs, his values and attachments? Changing beliefs is a rather complex task; before attempting to instil new values and 'facts' into people, the change agents often had to undermine the human personality and break down the existing belief systems and attitudes first. This complex task was often accomplished by exerting tremendous physical, intellectual and emotional pressure and appeals. Physical exhaustion and psychological coercion were combined with evangelistic exhortation, and these often led to confessions of past 'sins', such as admitting being a member of the 'exploiting classes' or being a heretic. These confessions can be seen as both a sign that the structures of the 'old' personality have collapsed and as a signal that the remaking or *re*-education of the 'new man' has started.

In thought reform programmes people are 'indoctrinated' or 'brainwashed', which means that they are subjected to methods that are aimed at the destruction of their beliefs, values, loyalties and attitudes. Brainwashing is an attempt to nullify the achievements of education and tradition, to transform the mind into a *tabula rasa*, after which the re-education and the 'closing' of the mind can take place. In brainwashing, according to the German psychologist Lersch, the *Abbau*, the breaking down of the ideological–mental, social and pragmatic frames, is followed by the *Aufbau*, the building up of other systems (1969). *Abbau* clearly indicates that (indoctrination as) brainwashing starts by putting out of action acquired dispositions, among others the critical attitude. Hence brainwashing requires the application of more forceful techniques than those that are needed to hamper the development of a critical attitude. *In the former case the victims are often rational people or adults, whereas in the latter the subjects are children or students who have the potential to become critical thinkers.*

Peters explains brainwashing as an effort to neutralize the person's capacity for choice. It is an attack on the individual's categoreal apparatus necessary for choice by making his environment as unpredictable as possible and by undermining his sense of time and place and his own identity:

> He is gradually reduced to a state of acute anxiety, perhaps of mental breakdown, in which he is in a receptive state to being dominated by another who becomes the sole source of pleasure and security for him. He becomes suggestible and willing to accept beliefs, which, in his former life, he would have rejected out of hand. He becomes more or less a programmed man rather than a chooser.
> (Peters, 1974, pp. 346, 347, 356)

After the annihilation of the critical disposition, inculcation of the doctrines can take place. In this sense '*re*-education' is a euphemistic term for indoctrination. The effects or the 'success' of miseducation is to a great extent dependent on the results of the 'washing of the brain', of the neutralization of the critical disposition, and one can seriously doubt whether this latter effort can ever be totally successful. Who could have expected that the (Berlin) Wall that divided Europe for almost thirty years, during which time the regimes had the opportunity to mould the minds of a whole new generation, would be broken down in 1989 because of mass protests of this same generation? The children in the DDR (East Germany) were taught in school that the Wall was nothing but a 'protection against imperialism', a safe *anti-faschistischer Schutzwall* (anti-fascist fence). All students over 14 had to take the course, *Wehrkunde* (Instructions on how to defend the 'socialist homeland'; this subject was officially abolished in December 1989). Many parents, however, abhorred the subject, especially the military exercises with toy guns and toy tanks. They also objected to the militaristic character of the school organization. Every class started with the same greeting ritual. One student stepped forward and addressed his fellow-students: 'Achtung, stillgestanden' (Attention!) The students jumped to attention, after which the class assignee stated: 'Sir, I declare the students to be ready for instruction.' The teacher in turn replied: 'Für Frieden und Sozialismus seid bereid' (Be prepared for peace and socialism). The students then replied with one voice: 'Immer bereit' (Always prepared) (cf. *NRC/Handelsblad*, 20 December 1989). The indoctrination and brainwashing of the students in school was apparently a stumbling-block for many parents, and this lack of backing from the parents, together with the population's ability to watch (news) programmes on West German television, partly explains why a peaceful political revolution was possible. The intellectual virtues which correspond to the (regulative) procedural rules somehow could not be sufficiently suppressed.

Brainwashing (or indoctrination in the second sense) is an expression of ideological totalism. All expressions of ideological totalism, according to Lifton (1962) in his study on brainwashing in China, are characterized by features or psychological themes which are predominant in the field of thought reform or re-education. Lifton's study on brainwashing can promote our understanding of indoctrination (in the first sense). Brainwashing is marked, among other things, by the features 'milieu control', 'mystical manipulation', 'demand for purity', 'sacred science', 'loading the language' and 'doctrine over person' (1962, pp. 420–35). I will explore to what extent these features can further our understanding of indoctrination (and of the analysis of 'indoctrination').

'Milieu control', or controlling human communication, is a basic feature of both forms of influencing people. In miseducation this can lead to deliberate isolation of children from dissentient peers, and to preventing the child from reading certain books or from watching television. In the first half of the twentieth century the social structure of Dutch society was (and in a certain sense it still is) marked by ideological compartmentalization (see Sturm, 1988). Broadcasting and educational systems in the Netherlands were (are) compartmentalized, as were journals, sports clubs and goat farming ('Goat Farming Association on Calvinistic principles'). Controlling information and communication, censorship in general (see Chapter 9 in this book, by Robin Barrow), of course prevents the beliefs of children from being shaken and the question of the validity of their beliefs from being raised.

The indoctrinator, like the brainwasher, justifies his actions by referring to his historical mission and to the 'Inexorable Laws of Historical Destiny' (Popper). He presents himself as the executor of the will of God, or as 'chosen' by a mystical force. The education of the child is nothing but a part of a 'mystical manipulation', in which the educator can only be an instrument.

In indoctrination the child is taught that the world (and also people) is sharply divided into pure and impure, into the absolute good and absolute evil ('the demand for purity'). The parent/indoctrinator conducts an all-out war against impurity in the child, and in this way promotes the disposition to have irrational feelings of guilt and shame—'irrational', because the cognitive core of these emotions is formed by doctrines that cannot be rationally justified. These doctrinal beliefs have an aura of sacredness ('sacred science'), and to exercise critical dispositions with reference to these basic dogmas is nothing but an act of desecration.

By the term 'loading the language' Lifton is referring to the way language is used to suppress a critical attitude. By using *thought-terminating clichés*, the indoctrinator hampers a reflective attitude to problems. Complex problems are compressed into highly reductive phrases ('capitalist bourgeois mentality'; 'abortion is murder'). Critical thinking is suppressed by presenting students with 'interpretative *shortcuts*', formulated in 'god terms' or 'devil terms' ('Aids is a punishment of God') (see Lifton, 1962, p. 429). The indoctrinator uses a language that is loaded with abstract jargon (sometimes in reference to only one domain) and that is highly judgmental. The child is, so to speak, linguistically deprived, and his potential capacities for critical thinking and rational emotions cannot develop.

'Doctrine over person' hardly needs further comment. 'Respect for the child as a person' is subordinated to the claims of the doctrines; the 'real' needs, wants and interests of the child are deduced from the doctrines. Only those who subscribe to the doctrines will be recognized as persons, while this right is denied to those who do not adhere to these beliefs.

FREEDOM AND INDOCTRINATION: CONCLUDING REMARKS

The term 'indoctrination', one can conclude, is closely connected with 'freedom'. Indoctrinating children, suppressing their critical disposition, necessarily implies that they are denied at least some forms of freedom. First of all, they are denied the right to develop into critical persons who can freely and fully participate in a democratic institution (marriage, church or political party) or state. Because their critical capacities will be crippled, they will not always be able to choose between critically assessed alternatives (cf. Steutel's 'autonomous' freedom). In this way they will not have the freedom to prefer one (moral or political) alternative to another, they often will be prisoners of rigid conventions (like sex roles), and at the same time be unable to discover the valuable aspects of a tradition. To cultivate the trait of reasonableness is 'to *liberate* the mind from dogmatic adherence to prevalent ideological fashions, as well as from the dictates of authority' (Scheffler, 1973, p. 142; my italics). At earlier stages of his development the child is denied the freedom to explore the world. Because of the strict control of his milieu and the lack of freedom of communication, the child is not free to satisfy his curiosity and also misses the opportunities to develop personal experiences and interests. Indoctrination also hampers the development of a free man or woman (cf. Peters), and can endanger an open society.

NOTE

(1)   This text is an extended and edited version of my (1987) 'Indoctrination, intellectual virtues and rational emotions' (*Journal of Philosophy of Education*, **21** (2), 261–6).
The author wishes to thank Jan Steutel and Johan Sturm for their incisive comments on an earlier draft.

REFERENCES

Beehler, R. (1985) The schools and indoctrination. *Journal of Philosophy of Education*, **19**, 261–72.

Green, Th. (1971) *The Activities of Teaching.* New York: McGraw-Hill.

Gregory, I. M. M. and Woods, R. G. (1972) Indoctrination: inculcating doctrines. In I. A. Snook (ed.) *Concepts of Indoctrination: Philosophical Essays*, pp. 162–90. London: Routledge & Kegan Paul.

Hare, R. M. (1972) Adolescents into adults. In R. M. Hare (ed.), *Applications of Moral Philosophy*, pp. 48–66. London, Macmillan.

Kazepides, A. C. (1973) The grammar of 'indoctrination'. In *Philosophy of Education 1973* (Proceedings), pp. 273–83. Worcester, MA: Heffernan Press.

Kohlberg, L. (1978) Moral education reappraised. *The Humanist*, Nov./Dec. 13–15.

Kohlberg, L. (1980) Stages of moral development as a basis for moral education. In B. Munsey (ed.) *Moral Development, Moral Education, and Kohlberg*, pp. 15–100. Birmingham, AL: Religious Education Press.

Kohlberg, L. (1981) *The Philosophy of Moral Development. Essays on Moral Development*, Vol. 1. San Francisco: Harper & Row.

Kohlberg, L. (1985) Resolving moral conflicts within the just community. In C. G. Harding (ed.) *Moral Dilemmas*, pp. 71–89. Chicago: Precedent.

Kohlberg, L. and Mayer, R. (1972) Development as the aim of education. *Harvard Educational Review*, **42** (4), 449–96.

Kohlberg, L., Levine, Ch. and Hewer, A. (1983) *Moral Stages: A Current Formulation and a Response to Critics.* London and New York: S. Karger.

Lersch, Ph. (1969) *Zur Psychologie der Indoktrination.* Munich: Verlag der Bayerischen Akademie der Wissenschaften, C. H. Beck.

Lifton, R. J. (1962) *Thought Reform and the Psychology of Totalism. A Study of 'Brainwashing'* in China. London: Victor Gollancz.

Michielsen, P. (1985) Denken verboden ['Thinking prohibited']. *NRC/Handelsblad*, 14 September.

Passmore, J. (1975) On teaching to be critical. In R. F. Dearden, P. H. Hirst and R. S. Peters (eds) *Education and Reason*. Part 3 of *Education and the Development of Reason*, pp. 25–43. London: Routledge & Kegan Paul.

Peters, R. S. (1974) *Psychology and Ethical Development*. London: Allen & Unwin.

Peters, R. S. (1983) Philosophy and education. In P. H. Hirst (ed.) *Educational Theory and its Foundation Disciplines*, pp. 30–62. London: Routledge & Kegan Paul.

Popper, K. R. (1982) Verdraagzaamheid en intellectuele verantwoordelijkheid. *Wijsgerig Perspectief*, **22**, (5), 144–9.

Sargant, W. (1957) *Battle for the Mind. A Physiology of Conversion and Brain-washing*. Melbourne, London and Toronto: Heinemann.

Scheffler, I. (1973) *Reason and Teaching*. London: Routledge & Kegan Paul.

Scheffler, I. (1977) In praise of cognitive emotions. *Teachers College Record*, **79**, 171–86.

Schein, E. H.(1956) The Chinese indoctrination program for prisoners of war. *Psychiatry*, **19**, 149–72.

Siegel, H. (1988) *Educating Reason. Rationality, Critical Thinking, and Education*. New York and London: Routledge.

Snook, I. A. (ed.) (1972) *Concepts of Indoctrination: Philosophical Essays*. London, Routledge & Kegan Paul.

Spiecker, B. (1984) The pedagogical relationship. *Oxford Review of Education*, **10**, 203–9.

Steutel, J. W. (1989) Over morele en intellectuele deugden. *Pedagogische Studiën*, **66**, (3), 107–18.

Sturm, J. C. (1988) *Een goede gereformeerde opvoeding. Over neo-calvinistische moraal-pedagogiek (1880–1950). Kampen: Kok*.

Thiessen, E. J. (1984) Indoctrination and religious education. *Interchange*, **15**, 27–43.

White, J. P. (1972) Indoctrination and intentions, and Indoctrination without doctrines? In I. A. Snook (ed.) *Concepts of Indoctrination: Philosophical Essays*, pp. 117–30, 190–201. London: Routledge & Kegan Paul.

Chapter 3

Indoctrination and Education[1]

Harvey Siegel

> In all education propaganda has a part. The question for the educator is not whether there shall be propaganda but how much, how organized and of what sort. . .[2]

> If you bring children up to think for themselves, it is not intelligible to say, in general, that you have indoctrinated them: because 'indoctrination' is opposed to 'thinking for oneself'. . .[3]

WHAT IS INDOCTRINATION?

If X's getting Y to believe that p is rightly thought of as X's indoctrinating Y into the belief that p, what must be going on with respect to X, Y and p? One view of indoctrination has it that the case is one of indoctrination if X's *aim* or *intention* is of a certain sort: namely, that X intends to get or aims at getting Y to believe that p, independently of the epistemic status of or evidence for p.[4] A second view holds that indoctrination is a matter of *method*, so that our putative case of indoctrination is a genuine one if X's method of getting Y to believe that p is of a certain sort: namely, one which tends to impart to Y a belief that p, independently of the evidence for p, and without Y's questioning p; a method, that is, which suppresses or discourages Y's critical consideration of the case for p (Smart, 1973, pp. 35, 42–3; Wilson, 1972 p. 19). A third view regards indoctrination as a matter of *content*, so that our case is a case of indoctrination if p is false or unjustified, independently of X's intentions and methods.[5]

I will not here try to analyse the dispute between these three views of indoctrination. For the three have in common a feature that serves well to distinguish indoctrination from other modes of belief inculcation. That feature concerns the *way* in which Y holds the belief that p. Our case is a case of indoctrination if Y believes that p in such a way that p's being held is not a function of evidence for p, and if evidence contrary to p is, for Y, irrelevant to the belief that p. Thomas F. Green, in an excellent discussion, puts the point in terms of Y's *style of belief*—our case is one of indoctrination if Y believes p *non-evidentially*, and X is best regarded as an indoctrinator if her aims, intentions or methods are such that they encourage a non-evidential style of belief:

> when, in teaching, we are concerned simply to lead another person to a correct answer, but are not correspondingly concerned that they arrive at that answer on the basis of good reasons, then we are indoctrinating; we are engaged in creating a non-evidential style of belief.
> (Green, 1972, p. 37)[6]

If a belief is held non-evidentially—that is, held without regard to evidence relevant to its rational assessment, and held in such a way that it is impervious to negative or contrary evidence—then the belief is an indoctrinated one, and the believer a victim of indoctrination. For the believer, in such a case, is incapable of critically enquiring into the worthiness of the belief. If a 'teacher' intends to foster such a non-evidential style of belief, or utilizes methods which tend to so foster, or seeks routinely to impart to students beliefs without regard to their truth or justifiability, and in so doing suppresses students' rational evaluation of said beliefs, then the 'teacher' is rightly regarded as an indoctrinator, and the student is a victim of indoctrination.

Students, in short, are indoctrinated if they are led to hold beliefs in such a way that they are prevented from critically enquiring into their legitimacy and the power of the evidence offered in their support; if they hold beliefs in such a way that the beliefs are not open to rational evaluation or assessment.[7] Indoctrination may be regarded as the collection of those modes of belief inculcation which foster a non-evidential, or *non-critical*, style of belief. For indoctrination, whatever else it may be, is *anti-critical*: it involves the holding of beliefs without due concern or regard for the evidential worthiness of those beliefs.

We see here, incidentally, that while intentions, methods and content are neither necessary nor sufficient for indoctrination, they can all tend to promote non-evidential belief. This is what is insightful about the three views of indoctrination noted, an insight incorporated in the view that indoctrination is a matter of non-evidential or *non-critical* belief.[8]

This is not the place for a full analysis of indoctrination. However, I believe that what has been said thus far is sufficient to suggest a fourth view of indoctrination, according to which indoctrination is not a matter of intentions, aims, methods or content, but rather a matter of the *results* or *upshot* of the aims, intentions, methods or content of instances of belief inculcation. If the teaching/learning interaction results in students' believing non-critically, or results in their developing non-evidential styles of belief, then the students are the victims of indoctrination. It is non-evidential, non-critical belief which is the hallmark of indoctrination, and such belief may or may not result from the teacher's aims or intentions, her instructional methods, or the content of that which is taught.[9]

IS INDOCTRINATION INEVITABLE?

Is it the case, as the epigraph to this chapter suggests, that education necessarily involves 'propaganda'? Is indoctrination inevitable? Many have argued for affirmative answers to these questions. Such arguments are often tangled up with a distinct question: is indoctrination always wrong or unjustified? If we think that indoctrination is never justified we might strive to show that indoctrination is avoidable; if, on the other hand, we think that indoctrination is sometimes justified, then we will not be concerned to deny the inevitability of indoctrination so long as *unjustified* indoctrination can be avoided.

Wilson suggests that the crucial question does not involve indoctrination, but the enhancement of rationality: 'The important point. . .is not so much whether we call something "indoctrination" or not, but whether a particular process increases or diminishes rationality" (1972, p. 21). If an educational process enhances rationality, on this view, that process is justified; if we choose to call it an indoctrinative process, then we have an educational process which is indoctrinative but nevertheless justified: a case of justified indoctrination (cf. Suttle, 1981).

What would such a case look like? Consider imparting to a young child the belief that reasons are important, and that acting on the basis of reasons is to be preferred to acting impulsively or without due consideration of the consequences of one's actions. Imparting this belief cannot be a matter of rationally convincing the child of its worth, for the child, in lacking the belief, has no reason (so to speak) for taking reasons offered on the belief's behalf seriously—*ex hypothesi*, she does not yet honour reasons or accept their force; consequently, giving reasons for the belief would be pointless. More importantly, the young child needs to learn what a reason is, and this, it seems, can surely not be learned by offering reasons for regarding certain things as reasons. The child must come to understand what a reason is before she can reasonably adopt a belief concerning the value of reasons, and such coming to understand cannot result from reasoning with the child. Yet adopting the belief in question will undeniably enhance the child's rationality. Here, then, we have a case which might be rightly regarded as a case of justified indoctrination—indoctrination because we get the child to adopt the belief in the absence of good reasons which she appreciates for adopting it; justified because the belief, adopted on whatever basis, enhances her rationality.

It would be so regarded, at any rate, if we are correct in calling this case of belief inculcation a case of indoctrination. Should it be so called? On some views of indoctrination, it should be. Paul Wagner, for example, defines indoctrination as 'causing a person to hold a belief which they [*sic*] are unable to justify on rational grounds' (1982, p. 192). For a variety of reasons, among them youth, inexperience, naivety and lack of knowledge, children—like the rest of us—may come to hold beliefs which they are unable to justify rationally. If this is the mark of indoctrination, as Wagner suggests, then indoctrination is indeed inevitable, and sometimes justified.[10]

It is undeniable, I think, that we seek to cause young children to hold beliefs in advance of their being able to rationally justify them. Parents and others spend quite a bit of time imparting to children a wide variety of beliefs—that they ought not to hit little sister, that they ought to share their toys with their friends, that they ought to avoid interacting with strangers, that Mummy and Daddy will protect them and so on—well before the children could give reasons for the beliefs, or even know what reasons are. We are agreed that such belief inculcation is desirable and justifiable, and that some of it might have the effect of enhancing the child's rationality. Should we call it indoctrination? This seems partly, at least, a verbal quibble. If we call it so, we are forced to give up the idea that indoctrination is always unjustified or evil, since we agree that some cases are justified. If we do not call such belief inculcation indoctrination, we preserve that term's pejorative flavour, but must give up Wagner's definition.

Clarity and educational theory are served, I believe, by taking the latter route. For, if the considerations of the last section are well taken, indoctrination involves primarily the style in which beliefs are held. Granting that many of the child's early beliefs are held in the absence of rational justification, we must distinguish between two crucially distinct cases: that in which the lack of justifying reasons is permanent and thought to be unobjectionable, and that in which it is temporary and tolerated only as a practical necessity. There is a world of difference between causing Johnny to believe things in such a way that they are now held *sans* rational justification, that he comes never to see the importance or relevance of enquiring into the rational status of his beliefs, and that it is thought to be unobjectionable that he never so comes; and causing Janie to believe things in such a way that they are now held *sans* rational justification, but with the view that this lack is tolerated only because it is temporarily necessary, and with an eye to imparting to Janie at the earliest possible time a belief in the importance of grounding beliefs with reasons and to developing in her the dispositions to challenge, question and demand reasons and justification for potential beliefs. In Janie's case, her independence of mind and the development of an evidential style of belief are taken to be central educational desiderata; her inculcation into unjustified beliefs is taken to be temporary, and, while practically necessary given her youth and cognitive situation, is to be replaced by justified beliefs as soon as possible. Calling Janie's case one of indoctrination, because it includes the inculcation of beliefs which she is at the moment unable to justify, obscures the fundamental difference between her case and Johnny's. For that reason it is best to reject the idea that all cases of belief inculcation in which the believer is unable to provide rational justification for the belief are cases of indoctrination. It is better to reserve the label for cases like Johnny's, in which the beliefs are inculcated without justification; in which that state of affairs is taken as unproblematic, and acceptable as permanent; and in which an evidential style of belief is discouraged, and a non-evidential style encouraged. In this way we distinguish *indoctrination* from non-indoctrinative belief *inculcation*.

Of course we could still see the question as largely a verbal one, and could still use 'indoctrination' to pick out cases like Janie's as well as Johnny's. We could do this as long as we distinguished in other ways between the two cases: in particular, if we considered cases of indoctrination to be justified if, like Janie's, they involved instances of belief inculcation *sans* justification only to the extent necessary for the further enhancement of rationality, and if they involved the development and encouragement of an evidential style of belief.

Granting, then, the necessity—both practical and conceptual—of belief inculcation in the absence of justification, we have good reason for not taking this to be the mark of indoctrination. Or, alternatively, if we do take this as the mark, then we must acknowledge that indoctrination is sometimes justified, and may enhance rationality.

Green takes it the latter way when he writes that

> Indoctrination has a perfectly good and important role to play in education. . .[and] may be useful as the prelude to teaching. . .we need not offer reasons for every belief we think important for children and adults to hold. On the other hand, we have no warrant to inculcate beliefs for which there is no good reason or for which we can offer no good reason, and we must be prepared to offer reasons or evidence when they are requested. . . .Indoctrination. . .may be sanctioned only in order that beliefs adopted may later be redeemed by reasons.
> (1972, pp. 44–5)

Here Green echoes Wilson in suggesting that the crucial question is the enhancement of rationality, and that indoctrination is justified in so far as it is necessary and causally efficacious for such enhancement. Taking 'indoctrination' as 'inculcating belief *sans* rational justification', I agree. But here Green curiously ignores his earlier emphasis on the desirability of the development of an evidential style of belief, and of a non-evidential style as the mark of indoctrination. Taking 'indoctrination' in this latter way, we should regard the cases being considered—cases in which beliefs are inculcated without rational justification, but in which those beliefs may later be 'redeemed by reasons', that is, given rational justification—not as cases of justifiable indoctrination but of non-indoctrinative belief inculcation. For in such cases beliefs are inculcated without rational justification only if (1) they help to develop in the believer an evidential style of belief, and (2) they are themselves to be 'redeemed by reasons', that is, the believer's belief in them without rational justification is regarded as temporary, and is to be replaced by belief which is rationally grounded. To consider such cases indoctrinative is to give up the idea that a necessary condition for holding a belief indoctrinatedly is not just holding it in the absence of rational justification, but holding it non-evidentially, so that reasons, evidence, and so rational justification are irrelevant to its being held. This seems an idea worth keeping. For one thing, it allows us easily to distinguish between the cases of Johnny and Janie. For another, perhaps more important: it is only with this notion of indoctrination that we can make sense of a belief's being 'redeemed by reasons'. If I believe that *p* non-evidentially, my belief cannot be redeemed by reasons, for in holding it non-evidentially I will not be moved by reasons for or against *p*. As Green himself puts it, 'beliefs held non-evidentially cannot be modified by introducing evidence or reasons or by rational criticism' (1972, p. 33). But if I believe that *p* without rational justification, but nevertheless have an evidential style of belief (or at least do not have a non-evidential style), I will be moved by reasons for *p*, and will happily redeem my previously adopted but ungrounded belief when I am able. In short, beliefs which are indoctrinated in that they are held without rational justification can be redeemed; beliefs which are indoctrinated in that they are held non-evidentially cannot. Given the central importance of such redemption, the importance of the enhancement of rationality, which requires such redemption, and the common sentiment, expressed by Wilson, that indoctrination and 'thinking for oneself' are contraries, we do better to regard indoctrination as involving, not simply beliefs held without rational justification, but beliefs held irrespective of such justification—that is, non-evidentially.[11]

   If the preceding paragraphs are correct, then Green has it nearly right, but not quite. For he should regard the inculcation of beliefs which are redeemable by reasons not as cases of sanctioned or justified indoctrination, but rather—since their redeemability implies the absence of a non-evidential style of belief—as cases of non-indoctrinative belief inculcation, in which reasons which justify the beliefs have not been passed on to the believer, but could have been, and in any case are in the possession of the inculcator. He should regard things in this way, that is, if he wishes his discussion of redemption to be consistent with his discussion of style of belief. For beliefs held without rational justification can be redeemed by reasons only if the believer is open to reasons and rational considerations which favour such beliefs. To be open in this way is to have an evidential style of belief (or at least not to have a non-evidential style). Such a case cannot consistently be regarded by Green as one of indoctrination, if he wishes to maintain his analysis of indoctrination in terms of style of belief (which, as I argued earlier, there are good reasons for maintaining). This is why the passage cited above cannot be quite right. On the 'style of belief' analysis of indoctrination, there can be no such thing as a belief which is indoctrinated yet redeemable—for if it is redeemable, then the believer must not have a non-evidential style of belief, in which case the belief cannot be an indoctrinated one. (To put the point in terms of an economic metaphor: the currency of redemption—reasons—has no purchasing power in a non-evidential economy.) In short: if indoctrinated, the belief cannot be redeemable; if redeemable it cannot have been indoctrinated.[12]

But the important point lies elsewhere. It is, to repeat, that, however one parses 'indoctrinate', it nevertheless remains the case that indoctrination is not unavoidable or inevitable in any sense in which it prevents the development of rationality.

A FURTHER DIFFICULTY?

One might think that a problem still remains. For how, specifically, can a child be brought to embrace unindoctrinated beliefs, in the absence of the capacity to judge the extent of reasoned support those beliefs enjoy? It seems undeniable that, however the child is brought to embrace early beliefs, in so far as the child lacks the concept of reasons and lacks an understanding of reasons and their force in justifying potential beliefs, her embrace will be non-rational. It is crucial for the enhancement of the child's rationality that we get the child to embrace non-rationally a belief in the power and value of reasons. To that extent, a critic might seem within her rights to insist that, despite what has been said thus far, it nevertheless remains that the child must be indoctrinated into the beliefs constitutive of the commitment to rationality. How, then, can we get the child to appreciate reasons, and adopt the belief that it is a good thing to believe and act in accordance with reasons, except by indoctrination? As Suttle poses the problem: 'if educators desire students to believe that they ought to want to develop and utilize their rational capacities, then educators may very well have to indoctrinate the students in this belief' (1981, p. 155).[13]

R. S. Peters puts the problem, which he refers to as the 'paradox of moral education', in this way:

> given that it is desirable to develop people who conduct themselves rationally, intelligently and with a fair degree of spontaneity, the brute facts of child development reveal that at the most formative years of a child's development he is incapable of this form of life and

impervious to the proper manner of passing it on.
(1966, p. 252).

Since the child is at this stage 'incapable of [the rational] form of life', she cannot be brought to it by rational means. How, then, *can* she be brought to it? According to some, only by way of indoctrination (cf. Suttle, 1981, pp. 156–7; Wagner, 1982).

A classic answer to the paradox of moral education appeals to *habit*. As Peters puts it, echoing thinkers as diverse as Aristotle and Dewey,

> in spite of the fact that a rational code of behaviour and the 'language' of a variety of activities is beyond the grasp of young children, they can and must enter the palace of Reason through the courtyard of Habit and Tradition.
> (1966, p. 253)

Does the development of proper habits allow us to escape the paradox, and inculcate a commitment to rationality without indoctrinating children into that commitment? It does, if it be granted that habits can themselves become criticizable. If we develop in a child the habit of searching for reasons which justify a potential belief before adopting the belief, that habit not only enhances her rationality. It also admits of rational evaluation itself, for the child can (and we hope will) question the reasons which recommend that habit as a worthy one, and assess the force of those reasons herself. The development of rational habits, then, does not require either indoctrination or the forsaking of rationality. Rather, such development simply helps us to impart to children traits we believe desirable, in the face of 'the brute facts of child development'.

Grant that we inculcate, at first, *sans* reasons. In doing so, it is hoped, we transform the child from one who cannot appreciate and be moved by reasons to one who can; from a pre-rational person to a rational one. To focus on *how* the transformation is accomplished, however, is to focus on the wrong concern.[14] The important question is not 'How is the transformation accomplished?'—admittedly, it is accomplished by non-rational means in that the child is not rationally persuaded to become rational—but rather, 'Does the transformation, however accomplished, enhance the child's rationality and foster an evidential style of belief?' If the answer to this latter question is affirmative, then we need not fear the charge of indoctrination. To label the development of early beliefs and habits 'indoctrinative' is to take indoctrination to be the inculcation of beliefs which the believer cannot rationally justify. Earlier we saw the problems attending this conception of indoctrination. On a preferable conception—which takes indoctrination to be largely a matter of the style in which one holds beliefs—early belief and habit inculcation is not indoctrinative, so long as the beliefs and habits inculcated enhance the child's rationality, foster an evidential style of belief, and admit of rational justification which the child is encouraged to seek, grasp and use to 'redeem' the previously inculcated beliefs and habits as soon as she is able. Thus we may grant the inevitability of early inculcation of beliefs and habits in the absence of rational justification, without running afoul of the indoctrination objection. The fostering of rationality may proceed in the absence of a damning or damaging indoctrination.

THE RIGHT TO AVOID INDOCTRINATION

What is so awful about indoctrination, anyway? Supposing that the argument advanced thus far succeeds, and indoctrination is avoidable, why should we avoid it?

If I have been indoctrinated, and so have developed or had fostered in me a non-evidential style of belief, I have been significantly harmed. My autonomy has been dramatically compromised, for I do not have the ability to settle impartially questions of concern to me on the basis of a reasoned consideration of the matter at hand. I am in an important sense the prisoner of my convictions, for I cannot decide whether my convictions ought to be what they are, and I am unable to alter them for good reasons, even if there are good reasons for altering them. Indeed, lacking the disposition to seek reasons, I am doomed to an unawareness of the desirability of aligning my beliefs and actions with the weight of relevant evidence. Consequently, my life is limited; options with respect to belief and action—and indeed of basic aspects of my life-style and beliefs about the worthwhile life (if I have any)—are forever closed to me, owing to my antipathy towards the contemplation both of challenges to my unreasoned but presently held convictions and of alternatives to them. I have been trapped in a set of beliefs I can neither escape nor even question; this is how my options, and my autonomy, have been limited. I have been shackled, and denied the right to determine, in so far as I am able, my own future. In being indoctrinated, I have been placed in a kind of cognitive strait-jacket, in that my cognitive movements have been severely restricted. Worse, like the typical strait-jacketed person, I have also been sedated—drugged—so that I don't even realize my restricted plight.[15] Such a limited life cannot be what we desire for our children, any more than we desire it for ourselves.

The child has an overwhelming interest in avoiding indoctrination. To be so shackled, and to have her options and future limited, is to narrow her life in a way which is as unacceptable as it is out of her control. In being indoctrinated, the child is cut off from all but a narrow band of possibilities. Her freedom and her dignity are short-circuited, her autonomy denied, her control over her own life and her ability to contribute to community life truncated, her mental life impoverished.[16] This is a more apt description of child abuse than of acceptable education. As we have a moral obligation to stand against child abuse, so we have a similar obligation with respect to indoctrination.[17]

A FURTHER ISSUE: THE POSSIBILITY OF INDOCTRINATION IN SCIENCE

Several philosophers of education have argued that it is not possible to indoctrinate in science. These philosophers (see Chapters 1 and 2 in this book) generally argue for this view by arguing that indoctrination necessarily involves doctrines—that is, a specific sort of content; that science has no such doctrines; and therefore that indoctrination is not possible in science. In this section I should like briefly to examine one such argument.

Ben Spiecker advances a view of indoctrination quite like the view I have defended above, according to which indoctrination involves belief which is 'screen[ed]. . .from criticism'; which involves the suppression of the 'critical dispositions of the students' indoctrinated; which 'begins when we try to stop the growth in our children of the capacity to think for themselves'; which 'involves the suppression of the disposition for critical reflection'; which 'still[s] critical reflection'; and which involves a systematic neglect of or indifference to relevant evidence and reasoned judgment (Spiecker, 1987, pp. 262–3). All this sounds quite like the account of indoctrination offered above in terms of non-evidential, non-critical style of belief. Why should it be thought that a person cannot be indoctrinated (in this sense) into scientific beliefs? Spiecker argues that scientific beliefs are immune to indoctrination because 'sciences. . .are constituted in principle by the rule that all propositions are to be tested on their validity' (1987, p. 262). Understood as the thesis that science is rational in that it is best characterized by a commitment to evaluating hypotheses in terms of evidence, I agree (cf. Siegel, 1985). But this view about science's 'constitution' and rationality is irrelevant to the way in which people hold scientific beliefs. I may believe something about quantum mechanics or natural selection because I have found it supported by relevant evidence; but I may also believe it in an entirely uncritical manner. The 'non-critical attitudes' which Spiecker (1987) (rightly, in my view) associates with indoctrination can be manifested with respect to scientific beliefs every bit as much as they can be manifested with respect to non-scientific beliefs. The same can be said for mathematical beliefs, or indeed any sort of belief. There is no area of curricular concern which is not susceptible to the dangers of indoctrination; no subject matter in which belief cannot manifest 'non-critical attitudes' or be maintained non-evidentially. In so far as indoctrination is rightly seen as a matter of non-critical or non-evidential belief, there is no particular sort of belief—scientific or any other—which is immune from the possibility of indoctrination.[18]

CONCLUDING CONSIDERATIONS

As has been argued, it is best not to regard all cases of belief inculcation *sans* rational justification as cases of indoctrination. It must be granted that we sometimes have no alternative but to teach children, or at least to inculcate beliefs, without providing them with reasons which serve to justify those beliefs. For before we can pass along reasons which the child can recognize as reasons, she must come to understand what a reason is. Nevertheless, we can inculcate beliefs which enhance rationality, and help to develop an evidential style of belief. Such belief inculcation, even though it does not, of necessity, include the passing on of reasons which are seen by the believer as warrant for the inculcated beliefs, ought to be considered non-indoctrinative belief inculcation rather than indoctrination.

   If I get a young child to believe that the sun is 93 million miles from the earth (on average), that it is better to share her toys with her friends than not to share, that $2+2=4$, or that it is desirable to believe on the basis of reasons, I am not necessarily indoctrinating. I am indoctrinating only if I pass on these beliefs in such a way that the child is not encouraged to, or is prevented from, actively enquiring into their rational status—that is, if her rationality is stunted, and if she is brought to develop a non-evidential style of belief.[19] If we inculcate beliefs *sans* reasons, but encourage the development of rationality and an evidential style of belief, we are not indoctrinating. We cannot start out giving reasons, for the child has to learn what a reason is, and what counts as a good reason—that is, the child has to learn how to evaluate reasons—before giving reasons even makes sense.[20] Consequently, we have no choice but to begin by inculcating beliefs in the absence of justifying reasons. But this should not blind us to the central distinction between doing so as a necessary prelude to the development of rationality and an evidential style of belief, and doing so without regard to such further development. Only the latter is appropriately considered indoctrinative. We avoid indoctrination by taking the former path: by encouraging the student to become our 'critical equal' and assess for herself the strength of the support which reasons offer for inculcated beliefs; to subject reasons which we take as justificatory to her independent judgement; and to transcend her intellectual dependence on us and drive, ever more competently, her own doxastic engine. We avoid indoctrination, in short, by taking seriously—even as we inculcate beliefs, as we sometimes must, in the absence of reasons which justify those beliefs—the educational ideal of rationality/critical thinking.

NOTES

(1)   This chapter is a modestly revised and extended version of Chapter 5 of my *Educating Reason: Rationality, Critical Thinking, and Education* (1988).

(2)   B. Russell quoted by Smart (1973, p. 33).

(3)   Wilson (1972, p. 23)

(4)   Snook puts it this way: 'A person indoctrinates P (a proposition or a set of propositions) if he teaches with the intention that the pupils or pupil believe P, regardless of the evidence' (cited in Smart, 1973, p. 39). See also Wilson (1972, pp. 18–20) and Spiecker (1987), both of whom endorse the idea that indoctrination is necessarily intentional. But Wilson seems to hold in these pages that indoctrination is also, necessarily, a matter of method and content as well, while Spiecker holds that it is a matter of content.

(5)   Cf. the discussion of the relation between indoctrination and truth in Green (1972). Flew (1966) conflates the first and third views mentioned when he writes that indoctrination is a 'matter of trying to implant firm convictions of the truth of doctrines which are either false or at least not known to be true' (cited in Benedict-Gill, 1981, p. 104). Cf. also Wilson (1972) and Spiecker (1987).

(6)   Green, putting the point in terms of aims, writes that 'Indoctrination aims simply at establishing certain beliefs so that they will be held quite apart from their truth, their explanation, or their foundation in evidence' (1972, p. 25); he explicates the notion of 'non-evidential belief' in this way: 'When beliefs are held without regard to evidence or contrary to evidence, then we may say they are held non-evidentially. It follows that beliefs held non-evidentially cannot be modified by introducing evidence or reasons or by rational criticism' (p. 33). Cf. also Green (1971, pp. 48–51); here too Green characterizes indoctrination in terms of aim or intention.

(7)   As Wilson puts it, in his excellent phrase, indoctrinated beliefs are those which have been accepted when the indoctrinated person's 'will and reason have been put to sleep' (1972, p. 18).

(8)   Thus intention is neither necessary nor sufficient for indoctrination, contrary to many authors (see, for example Spiecker, 1987): if I do not intend to establish beliefs irrespective of the evidence for them, but nevertheless my students wind up with non-evidential styles of belief, then we should still say that they have been indoctrinated, and

that I (however unwittingly) indoctrinated them by fostering such styles. Uncriticality and non-evidential beliefs, not intention, are the marks of indoctrination.

(9) Neiman (1989) usefully discusses the indoctrination debate and in so doing, makes plausible a position quite close to the 'upshot' account of indoctrination just defended. Neiman's discussion makes clear that rationality is an educational ideal shared by the proponents of all the major accounts of indoctrination. While I do not endorse Neiman's advocacy of 'contextualism', I do endorse his arguments for the respectability of a results-oriented account of indoctrination; he is also correct in locating rationality at the heart of the indoctrination debate. I hope that the account of indoctrination offered here adequately reflects the centrality of rationality both to that debate, and as an educational ideal.

(10) Cf. also Suttle (1981). These questions and related ones concerning indoctrination and moral education are fruitfully pursued in the exchange between Pincoffs and Baier (see Baier, 1973).

(11) Note that this solution has the ramification—positive, if one favours consistency with ordinary language—of preserving the pejorative connotation of 'indoctrination'. I hope it is clear, however, that considerations of ordinary usage play virtually no role in my argument. The important thing is not to offer a conception that adequately captures our intuitions about indoctrination or our uses of 'indoctrination'. The important thing, rather, is adequately to determine that which our educational institutions ought to be about. Hard philosophical work concerning the aims of education and their justification (and harder empirical work aimed at making those philosophical aims and ideals reality) far outstrips the analysis of ordinary language that for so long strangled analytic philosophy of education.

(12) As Denis Phillips points out, this implies that if a person has been indoctrinated, that indoctrination cannot be undone *by appealing to reasons*, since she has a non-evidential style of belief. Counteracting indoctrination, I think, requires not the alteration of specific beliefs, but the development of an evidential style of belief. This must be the aim of 'dedoctrination'.

(13) Despite our disagreement over the inevitability of indoctrination, our views concerning both moral education and the place of rationality in education are in many respects quite close. I am grateful to Suttle for extensive and very helpful correspondence and conversation on these and related issues.

(14) Consequently it does not matter much to my argument whether Aristotle, Dewey and Peters are right concerning the role of habit in the resolution of the paradox of moral education. I believe that they are, but the argument for the possibility of inculcating beliefs and habits *sans* rational justification without that inculcation constituting indoctrination goes through even if habit is not the key to the resolution of the paradox. Note also that we are here considering how one *becomes* rational, rather than what it is to *be* rational. These two matters being distinct, I hope it is clear that my Kantian answer (cf. Siegel, 1988) to the latter does not conflict with my (weakly) Aristotelian answer to the former. Here I am grateful to Dennis Rohatyn.

(15) As Smart (1973, p. 45) puts it, 'to be indoctrinated is to be enmeshed within a web of doctrines from which there can be no escape. One cannot extricate oneself because one sees no need for doing so. Usually we change our opinions in the light of experience or because of inconsistencies which arise from commitment to particular beliefs. But if we are presented with a set of beliefs which can explain away alleged inconsistencies and maintain that experience is irrelevant there remains nothing which can challenge our beliefs.'

(16) As Wilson (1972, p. 22) puts it, 'To indoctrinate is . . . to take over [the child's] consciousness.'

(17) As I suggest (in Siegel, 1984), much fundamentalist religious education fits this indoctrinative, immoral picture, and children have a right to be protected from being victimized by such an education, even though it may be private rather than public education—and we have a concomitant obligation to so protect them. Green suggests a similar view of the character of fundamentalist religious education (1972, pp. 40–1).

(18) Moreover, any 'doctrine', however this notion is conceived, can be believed either evidentially or non-evidentially. So 'doctrines' won't serve as the key to understanding indoctrination, while evidential/non-evidential style of belief will. For further discussion of the way in which science education can be indoctrinating, see Siegel (1988, Chapter 6).

(19) There is a neat self-referential problem with the last belief mentioned, which solution may require that that particular belief *cannot*, in principle, be the object of indoctrination. We need not settle the question here.

(20) This sentence, and other ideas of this and the preceding paragraphs, are taken from Siegel (1980).

REFERENCES

Baier, K. (1973) Indoctrination and justification. In J. F. Doyle (ed.) *Educational Judgements*. London: Routledge & Kegan Paul.

Benedict-Gill, D. (1981) Some philosophical directions in a controversy over public moral education. In C. J. B. MacMillan (ed.) *Philosophy of Education 1980: Proceedings of the Thirty-Sixth Annual Meeting of the PES*. Normal, IL: Philosophy of Education Society.

Flew, A. (1966) What is indoctrination? *Studies in Philosophy and Education*, **4** (3), 281–306.

Green, T. F. (1971) *The Activities of Teaching*. New York: McGraw-Hill.

Green, T. F. (1972) Indoctrination and beliefs. In I. A. Snook (ed.) *Concepts of Indoctrination*. London: Routledge & Kegan Paul.

Neiman, A. M. (1989) Indoctrination: a contextualist approach. *Educational Philosophy and Theory*, **21** (1), 53–61.

Peters, R. S. (1966) Reason and habit: the paradox of moral education. In I. Scheffler (ed.) *Philosophy and Education*, 2nd edn. Boston: Allyn & Bacon.

Pincoffs, E. L. (1973) On avoiding moral indoctrination. In J. F. Doyle (ed.) *Educational Judgments*. London: Routledge & Kegan Paul.

Siegel, H. (1980) Rationality, morality and rational moral philosophy: further response to Freeman. *Educational Philosophy and Theory*, **12** (12), 41–2.

Siegel, H. (1984) The response to Creationism. *Educational Studies*, **15** (4), 360–2.

Siegel, H. (1985) What is the question concerning the rationality of science? *Philosophy of Science*, 52 (4), 517–37.

Siegel, H. (1988) *Educating Reason: Rationality, Critical Thinking, and Education*. London and New York: Routledge.

Smart, P. (1973) The concept of indoctrination. In G. Langford and D. J. O'Connor (eds) *New Essays in the Philosophy of Education*. London: Routledge & Kegan Paul.

Spiecker, B. (1987) Indoctrination, intellectual virtues and rational emotions. *Journal of Philosophy of Education*, **21** (2), 261–6.

Suttle, B. B. (1981) The need for and inevitability of moral indoctrination. *Educational Studies*, **12** (2), 151–61.

Wagner, P. (1982) Moral education, indoctrination and the principle of minimizing substantive moral error. In D. R. DeNicola (ed.) *Philosophy of Education 1981: Proceedings of the Thirty-Seventh Annual Meeting of the PES*, Normal, IL: Philosophy of Education Society.

Wilson, J. (1972) Indoctrination and rationality. In I. A. Snook (ed.) *Concepts of Indoctrination*. London: Routledge & Kegan Paul.

Chapter 4

Religious (Moral, Political, etc.) Commitment, Education and Indoctrination

John Wilson

Problems about freedom and indoctrination surface in many departments of life and of education. I have chosen to tackle them in the area of religion, because their temperature there is apt to be highest and their difficulties to seem most intractable; but I use my somewhat cumbersome title just to make the point that the problems do not occur only in the field of religious education—though they may be most obvious there, and most obviously backed by particular institutions or organizations (for example the Christian churches). Individual teachers, parents and others, and social groups, will clearly have strong views in departments labelled 'moral', 'political', and—less obviously but offering a useful parallel—'aesthetic'. (Think of the views of the followers of F. R. Leavis; or, more simply, of educators who have very strong opinions about children's dress, hair-style and so on.) All this should remind us first that there are difficulties with the categories themselves—about what is to count as 'religious', 'political', and so on; and secondly that, for this reason if for no other, we cannot start by assuming that religion is an *entirely* different kettle of fish.

TASKS FOR THE EDUCATOR: A COMPARISON

Perhaps some of the relevant points may emerge more clearly if we start in a less dramatic and impassioned field, and ask what a reasonable parent or other educator would do about children's dress or personal appearance. Instead of lining up two armies under the headings of 'commitment' and 'autonomous choice', we would want to say a number of different things, including the following:

The parent or educator might reasonably feel that this area, falling (I suppose) under the general title of 'aesthetics', was worth taking seriously—that it was worth undertaking some kind of education in or about the area. At the same time he might recognize that this view was in various ways questionable. Thus it might be held

(a)   by an extreme puritan for instance, that it was somehow wrong or dangerous for children (or adults) to think about their personal appearance at all, or more than minimally;

(b)   that no serious education (in one important sense of the word: see below) could, logically, be undertaken here, since there could be no rules, or principles, or criteria in virtue of which one kind of dress or appearance could be reasonably seen as better or worse than another—that the whole business was 'arbitrary' or 'a matter of taste' or 'relative', or something of that kind;

(c)   that the whole business, though not *per se* dangerous (as in (a)) or irrational (as in (b)), was just not in any way *important*; that children and adults could go through life perfectly well without reflecting seriously on it;

(d)   that it might be important for some children, less important or quite unimportant for others.

Suppose, nevertheless, that he reaches the conclusion that educators should take dress seriously. It is important to see that reaching this conclusion—the reasons and thoughts that back the conclusion—will be, not just necessary if the enterprise is to be justified, but an essential part of that enterprise itself. Whatever reasons there may be—and I am myself quite sure there are some—for supposing religion, morals, politics, aesthetics or whatever to be both necessarily important for the lives of all or most children, and subject to some kind of rational control, and hence to education, these reasons will have to be transmitted to the children if the education is to work properly. The children will have to see the *point* of the whole enterprise, and also to see that there is such a thing as *performing well or badly* in the area: just as children see why we need to do science (if, as we must, we need to know about the physical world) and how science works—how there can be principles and methods which can help us to sort the physical world out. Without this, the enterprise could be written off as either trivial (as one might think, for instance, about teaching children to speak in this or that accent and pronunciation), and/or non-rational (as with astrology). So the educator would have to start by getting these reasons clear, and thinking about how to make them clear to children.

He would then bump up against the (obvious) fact that there existed various *traditions* ('commitments') of dress and appearance, and distinguish the points:

(a)   that he himself, perhaps also the rest of his family or social group, was 'committed' to a particular tradition, and that it would be impossible (short of going around naked) to conceal this from the child;

(b)   that—again, short of not dressing the child at all—the child would have to be 'brought up in a particular tradition', that is, dressed in a certain style, at least in her early years when the question could not be negotiated with her;

(c)   that there were, nevertheless, and particularly in a pluralist society with good communications between social groups, many *different* traditions from which the child could not be shielded (or not for long);

(d)   that one important feature of these traditions consisted, not so much in their value *per se*—in having achieved 'good' dress and appearance—but (also) in their representatives (fashion houses, dress designers, hair stylists) having reflected on, experimented and in general rationally considered dress and appearance as subjects of study; briefly, that the traditions incorporated educationally desirable elements—reflections about colour clashes and combinations, style and so forth—as well as propounding particular 'answers' to questions about dress;

(e)   that some traditions, perhaps partly because of the points made in (d), might be better than others as a basis on which to educate children. Some for instance might be less 'closed' than others, allowing and encouraging opportunity for further development and reflection; some again might give the child a certain basic security about dress (might school uniform do this?) so that the child would feel sufficiently confident, not too anxious or surrounded by too much variety, to progress towards rational choices of her own.

The educator/parent would also realize that these traditions themselves would, almost inevitably and surely correctly (since the value of any tradition must ultimately rest upon certain *reasons*), come up in the child's mind for assessment and criticism; so that it could not be sufficient merely to educate the child in accordance with a single tradition, or even give her experience of many traditions. The child would need to be taught how to *judge between* different traditions: to be taught the criteria by which such judgements could properly be made. Indeed, it would not be clear just what value lay, *per se*, in educating her within one or more traditions, since (as I have said) the value of any such tradition would rest at least partly on the reasons which lay behind it. So he would try to see how the child could be taught the basic principles that lay behind *any* such tradition: the 'form of thought' (knowledge, experience), presumably 'aesthetics', which the tradition formed a *part of*. Whether or not he reserved the term 'education' for this, perhaps more advanced or critical, type of teaching and learning might not matter very much; but he would recognize the *difference* (not necessarily the *conflict*) between teaching the child how to dress in a certain way on the one hand, and teaching her how to adjudicate on or criticize various ways of dressing on the other. In particular, he would appreciate the difference of *authority* or *expertise* in these two matters. If we teach children to understand and habituate themselves to (say) dressing as fashion models or businessmen, the authorities for that stand within those particular traditions; but if we teach them to criticize these traditions, the only authority is the authority of whatever principles of thought and criticism stand behind *all* traditions—to put it grandly, the transcendental principles of reason or rational aesthetics; or, less grandly, the insights, methods of thought, types of argument, perceptual ability and (in general) the mental equipment which will enable the child to make good practical judgements about dress or appearance.

The same considerations apply fairly obviously to, for instance, musical appreciation. We should have first to think that music was important enough to be worth educators' attention. Then we should have to grasp just why it was important, and what counted as appreciating well or badly (or not at all). Thirdly, we should recognize the existence, and diverse merits, of different types of music (Western classical, Indian, pop and so on), and inevitably (a) and (b) bring the child up in one, or at most a few, traditions—we could not bring her up in all at once; but recognizing (c), (d), (e) that some traditions were to be preferred on educational grounds, not just because they were current with us. Finally we should have to think harder about how to help the child appreciate or adjudicate between different traditions (and musical compositions within one tradition).

CAN THESE TASKS BE PERFORMED?

It is worth asking what prevents us from following this procedure or set of tasks. It is not sufficient to say that each of us is so firmly wedded to a particular tradition, so committed to his or her own beliefs, that we resist this idea of there being general criteria of reason which stand above and beyond them all; for, in most pluralist and liberal societies at least, many of us would in principle welcome the idea—if only because of our fears about indoctrination, or our recognition that young people will in fact meet competing traditions. Our difficulties operate at a higher level, in a way I will try to describe briefly.

In a way it is precisely our acknowledgement of pluralism that constitutes our problem. Many philosophers who write about religion are concerned more with different religions than with religion as any sort of *sui generis* enterprise. It is as if we thought, not only that particular religions differed, but also that the very concept of religion could not be clearly demarcated—not clearly enough, at least, to pursue the further and connected question of what criteria applied to anything that could seriously be called 'religion'. Some philosophers are frightened of what is sometimes called 'essentialism'—the idea that there must be one single thing common to all cases of religion—or have other doubts and fears about the business of 'defining' such enterprises. Others talk of 'contestable concepts', in a way which suggests that there could in principle be no such firm demarcation, since the concept of religion can change over time and space. Similar moves have been made with other concepts—those marked by 'education', 'morals', 'politics' and 'art' are often treated in much the same way. In general there is a strong resistance, at least quasi-philosophical, to the attempt.

I have tried elsewhere (Wilson, 1986) to deal with this fully, with particular reference to the concept of education (and see pp. 46–7); but it may suffice here to say that the question 'What are we going to talk about, when we talk about "religion" ("religious education")?' is surely a legitimate one. Certainly young people will raise this question, explicitly or implicitly; and certainly we cannot avoid answering it in some way, if only implicitly by our behaviour and practice in schools. In the past some of us answered along the lines of 'When I say religion of course I mean the Christian religion, and when I say the Christian religion of course I mean the Church of England.' But we ought to be able to improve on that. Maybe there are large and fuzzy areas, plenty of borderline cases, and multiple criteria for what to count as religion; maybe the problem calls for wise or judicious stipulation or decision (rather than for analysis of 'how the word is normally used'), though I do not think that is actually the case (Wilson, 1971). But at least something must be said.

It would not perhaps matter very much if we succeeded only in demarcating certain aspects of religion, and thereby gained some idea of how a rational individual should proceed in those aspects. A parallel might be found in moral education, where R. M. Hare and his followers (among whom, more or less, I count myself) have taken 'morality' to refer to a person's *overriding* principles and made a very tight connection between principles and behaviour. 'Morality', in so far as we can pin it down to one definition at all, certainly extends beyond that (there is, for instance, the whole business of how a person *feels* as well as what he *does*; and Hare does not say much about the ideals and general ways of life which may not entirely, or even largely, fall within the area perhaps better termed 'interpersonal morality'). But it is surely an important step forward to see how, on that (perhaps one-sided) demarcation of morality, moral education can get going.

Similarly in the case of religion, I have argued that the central questions—I think, all the specifically *religious* questions—are to do with the appropriateness of certain attitudes and emotions in reference to certain targets or objects, particularly the attitude of *worship*. If it is now said that some things we call religions (Buddhism in certain forms, perhaps) do not go in for worship, I shall not be much aggrieved; for it is, surely, an important question what (whom), if anything, a person ought to worship, and for what reasons; what criteria lie behind the allegiance, or reverence, or whatever he may give to (taking examples at random) Jesus, Hitler, a pop star or idol, the Koran, the Pope, the starry heavens above or the moral law within. If there are other questions which can reasonably be called 'religious' (as against, for instance, moral or historical or scientific), well and good; we must identify these and find out how a reasonable person would answer them.

One would have hoped, particularly after Paul Hirst's lucid (if, in the case of religion and morality, somewhat skeletal) delineation of various forms of thought or experience (Hirst and Peters, 1970) that the task of working out these criteria would have appeared as congenial and be enthusiastically undertaken. It is very striking (for an educationalist: those interested primarily in comparative religion may have other fish to fry) that this is not so, and that few people have even tried to give a clear account either of just what area we are talking about, or just what counts as a good performance in that area. Yet nobody believes that *nothing* counts. Worshipping Hitler (or whatever example the reader prefers) is some kind of *mistake*, a case of *unreason*. Very well: *what* kind? What did Hitler worshippers lack by way of essential equipment? How do we ensure our children have that equipment? What other mistakes and equipment are there? Not to face these questions is not to face the central problems of religious education at all.

COMMITMENT AND ASSESSMENT

Almost all commentators (that I know of) tend to miss some of these points, and gain plausibility only by pointing out that other commentators have missed others. Thus many commentators not unreasonably take exception to what is seen as too narrow a concept of education advanced by Hirst, and claim that the theologian has not only a right but a duty to speak about what education is and to make 'a distinctive contribution'; this because religion, as they say, 'is not a matter of logic'. But it is a matter of logic in one important sense: *not* in the sense, which has rightly upset many critics of the philosophy of education, that analysis of the *word* 'education' can compel certain educational practices; but in the sense that we all perfectly well recognize an enterprise that is *not* a matter of bringing the child up within a certain tradition and inducing 'commitment' to it but rather a matter of giving her the (non-sectarian) equipment to adjudicate between different traditions and commitments. This enterprise—whether or not we reserve the word 'education' for it—is, as I have been at pains to point out, not necessarily in *conflict* with particular traditions (only with those which include some refusal to undertake it), but it has different *aims*. (And because it has different aims, it will necessarily have different teaching methods.) The traditions and commitments, in this enterprise, will be *material for assessment*—including, of course, the teacher's own tradition and commitment; just as, to revert to my parallel, the teacher's own preferred dress and appearance can form the subject matter of criticism and analysis. This is, ultimately, a philosophical matter: it is (first and foremost) the business of determining what equipment the child needs to adjudicate and criticize. If any 'theologians' are concerned to determine this, then of course they can and should speak; but then they will have turned themselves into what it is clearer to call 'philosophers of religion (religious education)'. For they would then be making *no assumptions* about the merits or demerits of any tradition—even in the widest sense of deism, or theism, or life 'having a meaning', or the necessity to use certain kinds of (religious) language. In fact they would be unrecognizable as theologians.

The same points apply to the ablest defence of 'committed' religious education that I have seen (Mitchell, 1976). Very properly explaining the importance of bringing the child up in *some* tradition, Mitchell nevertheless thinks it is right, in a Christian school, 'to seek Christian commitment': hedging his bets somewhat not only by the rubric 'in a Christian school' but by phrases like 'not to bring undue pressure to bear on the individual' (*ibid.*). Similarly he hedges with political education, including among unexceptionable aims (such as 'an understanding of the intellectual basis of liberal democracy', and 'direct experience of working democratic institutions') the fence-sitting 'encourage a respect for human rights as these are understood in democratic societies'. This might (improbably) mean just that the child should understand something, but (almost certainly) means that the child should actually be brought to commit herself in some way, to have certain values and substantive beliefs about human rights. Even this might be all right, provided there is *also* a context in which the child is encouraged to criticize these commitments and consider other alternatives—*not* just for the sake of variety or to avoid indoctrination, which would produce a chaotic vacuum or shop-window tour of various ideologies, but because there must be an *uncommitted* context in which the transcendental principles of reason are allowed to operate on all or any particular ideology. Mitchell's readers might well doubt whether he actually believes that there are any such principles; he might (wrongly) be taken to think that traditions are, so to speak, all we have—that we have no external *points d'appui* from which to criticize them. This relativist position, certainly not Mitchell's, overtakes anybody who will not grant *some* space to uncommitted contexts of ratiocination and education.

It is of course possible to defend commitment as an aim, despite these arguments.

One defence is to interpret 'commitment' as a temporary phenomenon: to say that children should be encouraged to 'get on the inside of' particular religious (moral, political, aesthetic) beliefs or styles, in order to be able properly to adjudicate them; really 'getting the feel' of them rather than just hearing talk about them. Provided the children are *also* encouraged to emerge from these temporary 'commitments', that is unexceptionable; the only trouble is that this is not, surely, what most defenders of commitment mean by the word. Nobody suggests that to appreciate (for instance) music, one's critical or ratiocinative faculties must be working all the time—it is no doubt good tactics to suspend disbelief and sympathize, in as full a sense as possible, with what is placed before one. But one must also be able to step outside this sympathy and criticize.

Another defence (which I have not seen used) might be that the progress of the subject depends on having enough 'committed' people around, so that different points of view may be wholeheartedly expressed. Hence we might want to justify many different 'committed' schools who will produce different committed pupils who, as adults, will be able to join in the necessary dialogue. This plea for (full-blooded) pluralism seems to me more ingenious than plausible. The point is not just that it involves sacrificing individuals' rationality and rational education in order that we may retain them as full-blooded; it is rather that any serious dialogue needs individuals whose rationality is not thus sacrificed. We need people who can *both* sympathize as fully as possible with different points of view, *and* retain an identity and allegiance to pure reason which will enable them to engage in fruitful dialectic with other people: and that, as history abundantly proves, can only be done by a fairly intense process of education which emphasizes the rational as well as the committed. Of course I agree that rational dialectic is not achieved by individuals who—in an all too common liberal, anti-indoctrinatory, uncommitted and ultimately uninterested way—discuss religion merely for fun or for its peripheral sociological or other interest. But the commitment we need is the commitment to *truth* and to whatever equipment may be most relevant to getting at the particular kind of truth involved in religion. (This is what I tried to do in Wilson, 1971).

The only other defence (that I can see) is the Platonic one of maintaining the necessity, for reasons of social and individual harmony and security, of giving some or most children a ready-made 'faith to live by' *without* any real chance of criticizing it radically (and hence abandoning it). I do not at all deny that people, particularly children, need some kind of given structure to preserve them from anxiety and (if you like) 'make sense' of their lives. But it is a very open question what the contents or form of that structure should be; nor is it clear that it must involve metaphysical beliefs of any kind, let alone the particular beliefs of any one religion. I incline to the view that love, discipline and other such basic ingredients may be sufficient. But in any case, the defence would be dishonest if offered by most religious believers (including myself); it is one thing to sell Christianity because it is true, quite another to sell it as a useful social or psychological device. Nearly all Christians (that I know of) take the former view—and quite right too.

The fact is—to be practical—that children and more particularly adolescents will want to know *how to choose* between various options in religion, morals, politics, dress and many other things. Either we help them to do this (which includes, but is not included by, bringing them up within a tradition), or we do not. If we do, then we have to get down to the task of working out what equipment they need in these various areas, and determining how to give it them. That is, no doubt, not the only task of education, but it is difficult to think that, in the world as we have it or indeed in any conceivable world, it is not an important task. My objection to the defenders of 'commitment' is that they display no real understanding—because, perhaps, no real enthusiasm—of the nature of that task.

AN AUTOBIOGRAPHICAL EXAMPLE

Finally—since some of the above inevitably has a touch of polemicism about it—I should like to try to defuse or do more justice to some of the feelings which 'committed' people have. Unless this is done, we are likely to remain in antagonistic positions even after the logical ground has been covered. Perhaps I may be allowed to be autobiographical here, since the points lie somewhere at the interface between logic and feeling. I was brought up (the son of a minister of the Church of England) in a fairly orthodox Christian tradition, and went to schools where Christian ritual, liturgy and belief were strongly exemplified. From this I gained (at least as I see it) a number of different but important things, including an understanding (from the 'inside') of Christianity; a feeling of security and joy (something not often mentioned) from the tradition of corporate worship—the services, particular chapels and churches, hymns, prayers and so on; and (I hope) some important general insights—as much from things like parables and music as from doctrines—into what religion was about, what sort of light one religion at least might throw to someone interested generally in the human condition and human emotions. For all these reasons I should strongly resist any attempt to disband (so to speak) or dilute such an environment, particularly for the pseudo-reasons often advanced—that it is 'authoritarian', 'indoctrinatory' or whatever. In particular (as Mitchell has clearly shown) I should resist the idea that modern religious environments or educational traditions should be made more 'up to date', 'in tune with modern society', 'open ended' or (whatever this may mean) 'relevant'. For this tradition clearly has some, and some very important, merits; and we do not as yet know how to replace it with a better. It seems to me that modernists are simply frightened of the *power* which such a tradition exercises, and want to water it down; in this respect they are symptomatic of a more general loss of nerve in liberal societies, where we are very frightened of giving power to anyone or anything, preferring to dilute it and leave a vacuum rather than make proper use of its force. 'Modern society' should take its cue from religion rather than vice versa; and in this respect I should, I think, be inclined to be much more critical of contemporary Christian attitudes than most Christians would be.

At the same time my family and schools also, and without diluting my exposure to the Church of England tradition, offered me encouragement in the task of deciding for myself whether or not to be a Christian, what alternatives there were, and (most important of all) how a person might reasonably think and decide on such matters: encouragement which, unsurprisingly, led me into philosophy. My father would take me round different churches to gain experience (at least as important as just *talking* about alternatives); I listened to my elder brother (then in a Marxist phase); I would join in criticism of my father's sermons—criticism not necessarily confined to a Christian or even a religious basis—and so forth. Indeed, something also not commonly mentioned, the discussions and experience—conducted as they were in a context of love, trust and keenness to get at the truth—themselves provided me with much of the security, sense of identity and confidence that (like any young person) I needed. I should resist any attempt to dilute or remove all that, just as strongly as I should resist the other.

Briefly, it seems to me that we have here a common case: a case in which, for failure to make some (fairly obvious) distinctions, people tend to opt for *one* sort of regime, style or context at the expense of some other. The truth is surely that we have here two (or more than two) general tasks, each of which requires a 'powerful' context, and each of which—so far from conflicting—can support the other. It is just silly to ask whether a school should be committed to Christianity *or* to the impartial questioning and analysis of religion: like asking whether it should be committed to immersing children in Bach, Mozart, Beethoven and so on *or* to musical appreciation, to school uniform *or* to educating the pupils in dress and personal appearance. Briefly, not only in religion but also in morality, politics, aesthetics and indeed every form of thought and life both we and our pupils require *both* 'commitment' to a particular tradition and set of substantive values which will give them the psychological security they need (and is in any case inevitable); *and* 'commitment' to a form of thought and experience—itself a tradition, the tradition of Socrates—which stands above all other traditions and helps us to evaluate them. I have argued that the first kind of commitment should be chosen not just for its own sake, but with an eye to the second; and my claim is that, if understood in this sort of way, problems about freedom and indoctrination need no longer worry us philosophically. There remain, of course, psychological and other problems about how to give ourselves and our pupils the emotional security and backing necessary: briefly, how to give them not only a secure framework but also the ability to tolerate and enjoy doubt, questioning and the whole business of learning. I have said something about this elsewhere (1990); but much more remains to be said.

REFERENCES

Hirst, P. H. and Peters, R. S. (1970) *The Logic of Education*. London: Routledge & Kegan Paul.
Mitchell, B. (1976) Reason and commitment in the academic vocation. *Oxford Review of Education*, **2** (2).
Wilson, J. (1971) *Education in Religion and the Emotions*. London: Heinemann.
Wilson, J. (1986) *What Philosophy Can Do*. London: Macmillan.
Wilson, J. (1990) *A New Introduction to Moral Education*. London: Cassell.

Chapter 5

The Practice of Theory

Attila Horvath

In Hungary, one of the so-called East European countries, freedom in or of education has not played a significant role in theoretical discussions until very recently. It will be argued in this chapter that freedom in education is closely related to the general theory of freedom stemming from classical German philosophy. Although the concept of freedom has still not appeared in East European totalitarian educational systems, this does not mean that the communist ideology of schooling lacks philosophical foundations. The connection between Marxist conceptions of freedom and of communist praxis will be examined.

The issue of indoctrination is even more complicated since there is no Hungarian word for the concept and there is practically no literature dealing with the problem. Here I wish to show that communist ideology is dangerous not because it is evil and wishes to ruin people living under its rule but because it is self-deceiving and, despite its self-proclaimed materialism, does not want to face objective reality. For a proper understanding of what freedom and indoctrination might mean in our changing world the investigation of these concepts in previous East European theories and practices is inevitable.

Before we attempt to analyse the epistemological aspect of freedom and its relationship to indoctrination it might be useful to have a brief overview of the Marxist, or rather Eastern-Marxist, view of the concept. Marx used an historical and ontological methodology in his philosophical works and this may account for the lack of Marxist scientific enquiries into the criteria of freedom (in education). Marxist philosophers were more concerned with the genesis of freedom than with its everyday aspects, which, of course, would have been more problematic in the political sense. In fact Marx and Engels saw freedom as an infinite historical process rather than an aim to be achieved and thus provided their followers with ample ammunition to dismiss impatient questions, like 'Are we there already?'. Communism, like freedom, is not something that we strive for and then achieve and consume; it is a process of human development, a dialectical and historical phenomenon, and so static questions like 'Are we there already?' are irrelevant and disturbing. Communist parties in Eastern Europe made good use of this legacy and banned schools of thought other than the

Soviet-Marxist one. The lack of epistemological research impeded development of the critical analysis of existing circumstances and, in turn, left the theoretical-philosophical questions of education wholly to politics. Thus the question of freedom in education or in schools appeared to be a strictly political issue. For this reason philosophy of education, as such, does not exist in Eastern Europe. Aims, content and methods of education were seen as political problems. It is tempting to go into detail about the political practices of communism but a simplistic account of the horrors of the Stalinist era would say little about the subtle mechanisms of indoctrination. Instead, a short outline of the origins of the Marxist-Leninist conception of freedom may help.

Both Marx and Engels were proud of their philosophical antecedents and while they savaged the works of Feuerbach or Hegel their works drew heavily on the classical German schools of thought. What was common to Fichte, Hegel, Marx and Engels was that they all related freedom to necessity. Fichte saw individual freedom of the will as impossible in practice; he claimed that freedom of will is contrary to the very notion of education. He quite bluntly stated that freedom of the will is 'destroyed and swallowed up in necessity' (Fichte, 1968, p. 17). The aim of education, according to Fichte, is to produce 'strict necessity in the decisions of the will' and, most importantly, 'such a will can henceforth be relied on with confidence and certainty' (1968). This chilling definition of education means that the educator should arrange the learning environment in such a way that his aims in teaching will appear to the child to be unavoidable (natural) necessities, and the child, recognizing this necessity, will himself want to fulfil his teacher's aim. In short, education is a technique by which I indirectly make someone want what I want while he thinks that it is his will that is at work. In the light of what we know about the nature of indoctrination we can understand more clearly why the concept does not exist in East European theories of education; it has simply been dissolved in the notion of education itself, as German Romantic philosophy has exercised a strong and persistent effect on the culture of these countries. We can also see that this very special approach to the concept of education is not the result of communism. East European socialist states have simply been excellent homes for Fichtean thoughts.

Marx mainly relied on Hegel's more sophisticated philosophical basis to coin his conception of freedom. For Hegel, like Fichte, freedom was also the recognition of necessity: we do what we have to do. But according to him the extent of our freedom is shown by our understanding of the pressing necessities, as when in using the power of water to drive mills we employ the forces of nature—this recognition of natural necessity is a trick of the human mind. Marx and Engels used this line of thought in creating their conception of freedom. The distinction between humans and animals lies in their surroundings. Animals consume their environment and are subjected to the forces of nature. Even when they seem to create something it is not real work or conscious activity but biologically coded action. Human freedom starts with work and conscious, purposeful activity: freedom is to overcome and rule the powers of nature and also of society. Ruling and mastering social processes like those of the physical environment was the real breakthrough of Marxism, the results of which are well known in our history. Just as the flow of water could be detected (its direction, strength and so on) and by applying natural laws man could overcome his weakness and harness the powers of nature, so he could detect the laws of society and of historical development and use them to build a better world. Man must not be subjected to the caprice of natural or social forces which could be destructive. The level of planned and conscious shaping of the natural and social environment determines the degree to which humanity is free. No wonder that followers of Marx carefully avoided the question of individual freedom, since that had little importance in the ontogenesis of mankind. Freedom was of interest only in terms of the freedom of the human species; just as culture could not be seen in each and every individual despite the fact that it undeniably and objectively exists, so freedom might not be experienced by everybody despite the fact that it definitely exists for mankind. The expansion of freedom therefore, according to Engels, is possible only in socialism, which is the optimal context for becoming masters of our world:

> The circle of conditions of human life around mankind which ruled people now comes under the control and rule of men, who, for the first time, become conscious and real masters of nature. . . . They will with expertise employ the laws of their own social activities which until then were against them as alien natural forces.
> (Engels, 1975, p. 109)

As Marx and Engels wrote several times, until the rise of socialism history was something that had merely happened to mankind. The qualitative step towards freedom is to take an active role in shaping our world: 'The objective and alien powers which were ruling history now come under the control of man himself. . . . This is mankind's jump from the realm of necessity to the realm of freedom'(Engels, 1975, pp. 109–10).

Interestingly, the core of the Marxist concept of freedom was *control*. Both Marx and Engels, as well as their later interpreters, like the often quoted Davidov (1965), laid special emphasis on controlling our faith as a necessary condition for freedom. Control in their works remained on a theoretical, abstract level; they wrote about man, as such, controlling his environment but we find hints of more practical aspects in Marx's famous Eleventh Thesis on Feuerbach: 'Until now philosophers only interpreted the world; but the task for us is to change it' (Marx, 1960, pp. 365–7). All problems started here: in socialism Marx's abstract and ontological philosophical theorems were to be operationalized and applied to daily practice. With this shift from philosophical heights down to necessity, ruling, control and, consequently, freedom have gained new meanings.

By connecting the concept of freedom to natural necessities, laws and patterns of development Marxists created a solid basis for objective planning of not only the physical but also the social environment. If someone could not see the alleged freedom, they referred to another axiom which said that freedom is a social phenomenon and a continuous process, so if someone does not feel it then (1) it is there but the individual cannot see it, or (2) it is not there, but it is coming. Marxist epistemology having been based on materialism had to face the paradox of the mind being bound by the surrounding objective world while being able to change it at the same time. In theory this was possible by introducing dialectics, where something could be the result and the source of itself. In practice pluralism of ideas and views had to be eliminated because the laws of society's development are objective and so the task is to find the single, objective truth. This was done by introducing the term 'social consciousness' as a higher level of awareness than that of the individual. Consciousness, like culture or freedom, became an abstraction. The individual or groups in society could either recognize the laws of social development (contributing to the social consciousness), or could not because of the binding and blinding immediate circumstances. The former group gained freedom while the others remained the slaves of their own circumstances. Naturally this second group had consciousness as well, but it was *false* consciousness. We saw that neither for classical German philosophy nor for Marx did freedom mean free choice by free will from a list of divergent alternatives. Pluralism for them appeared to be the *vehicle* for finding ultimate truths in the teleological development of the universe. After all, freedom's faith must be bound by necessity (Davidov, 1965).

Marx wrote about the control of mankind over itself in general terms, but in reality somebody had to do the job. Necessity had to be impersonated by those able to recognize it. When this is done, again *somebody* must decide what is real and what is false consciousness and in real socialism this could only be done by the leading force in society, the Party. While in theory dialectical materialism was applied, in practice almost Fichtean subjective idealism stormed society. In the effort of proving communism's superiority over capitalism Fichte's proverbial axiom ruled everyday activity: if facts do not comply with theory—that's too bad for the facts. The practice of theory turned into an Orwellian *danse macabre*. This split between the theory and the practice of Marxism was the reason why so many of the critics of communist regimes in Eastern Europe started out as devout Marxists. For many it seemed (for a long time) that the theory was excellent; only its practical execution was at fault. It just had to be done well. We can find this illusion in the recent reform movements in Eastern Europe with slogans such as 'socialism with a human face'. By now it has become clear that the idea of revolutionary change, forcing a philosophy on to reality, is inherently inhumane. An analysis of how indoctrination functioned in our society might throw light on how freedom has been curtailed.

Indoctrination is clearly a more complex phenomenon than deliberately forcing children to chant political slogans which are not rationalized. This view of indoctrination is rather journalistic and lacks proper consideration of real cases of indoctrinatory practices for two main reasons. First, this definition cannot make distinctions between learning the national anthem and parrot-like reproduction of other, indoctrinatory material. In some circumstances, naturally, rote learning of the national anthem might be a tool for indoctrination but the above set of criteria fails to distinguish these further circumstances. Secondly, it is of paramount importance to treat separately the intentions, plans and strategies of political systems and of educators from what actually happens in classrooms. For if the system had really been indoctrinatory in Eastern Europe how could the dramatic changes of 1989 have happened? After all, one might wonder, were not the East European educational systems nurturing critical thinking more effectively than schools of any other democracies?

A further difficulty with the analysis of the concept of indoctrination is that no country or educator accepts the label. Just as all countries which have signed the international agreements and declarations on human rights violate the words and spirit of those documents, all political systems offer freedom and reject indoctrination in their schools, yet fail to put this into practice. While different religions and/or atheism are proudly advertised, the term 'indoctrination' seems to have become a philosophical four-letter word. This situation makes theoretical debate extremely difficult and helps to explain why philosophers of education love to refer to Nazi Germany or Stalin's empire. It seems that without these terrors of history theoretical investigations into indoctrination in the field of education would be greatly hampered.

Indoctrination is effective when the scope of values, concepts and meanings or, in general terms, of the elements of social discourse narrows. It works when people ask fewer and fewer questions not because it is forbidden (that would be sheer aggressive oppression) but because the list of questionable things is curtailed. More and more things in society are taken for granted or unalterably set. The question that immediately arises is evident: how wide should be the range of unquestioned things around us, when seeking the optimal number of taken-for-granted values? No one could seriously consider it necessary to examine everything around us with a critical mind; the debate starts when someone starts to list the unexaminable issues. It is obvious that we go out to certain public places (beaches) without clothes when it is hot and not to other places (streets). It is, however, less obvious whether one accepts that this choice should be controlled, or enforced by police or other authorities, or not. In schools when the teacher boldly encourages children to ask whatever they wish, he or she would nevertheless determine the range of questions considered 'valid'. Some would be 'off the topic', some others would 'make no sense', while there would be a few of the 'how dare you' types of enquiry which would be rejected by even the most open-minded educator. Control of freedom does not necessarily narrow the number of answers to a definite question; it may instead limit the number of acceptable questions. Which question is valid and which is not is largely dependent not only on the capacities of a given teacher but also on the rules of the culture he or she is working in. Some cultures are traditionally more open than others but to say that less open societies practise indoctrination more than others would be dangerous and not borne out by observation. Many would agree that education in revolutionary Iran is indoctrinatory but fewer would say the same about Japan's strict schooling techniques. Or why should we see ancient Chinese education as the proud product of thousands of years of wisdom (unquestioned), yet call communist China's schools the hotbeds of indoctrination? These questions force us to narrow the meaning of indoctrination: it is the deliberate action of changing and increasing the number of unquestioned things in a given culture. It is this active nature of indoctrination that constitutes the difference between teaching in an organically traditional, static society and an indoctrinating school system. The concept of indoctrination in this way connects with the Marxist conception of freedom. We saw that Marx and his followers advocated an active and purposeful changing of our social environment; they radically and rapidly wished to put things and thoughts into order. This aggressive shaping of things inevitably leads to indoctrination; the order of organically developed values must be upset and then rearranged, and in order to prevent the restructuring of values in accordance with the old order, the new rule must be maintained by force. Maintenance must mean keeping the new order stable (as Fichte demanded) and narrowing the range of challenging questions.

Indoctrination is the manipulation of 'human software' when the rules of treating facts and the rational arrangement of facts are changed. Expanding the range of unquestionable things in society is *de facto* indoctrination and this might be light years away from intended, legalized *de jure* indoctrination. This is why so many critical minds were able to emerge from the 'Eastern bloc'—they were living proof of a badly working indoctrinatory education. At the same time there are enormous difficulties in all former socialist countries in making people understand how a market economy works—and this is not because they are uneducated. Quite the reverse: they were so effectively 'educated' that they now have to learn a completely different set of rules. The problem for the academic arises when he wishes to detect indoctrination. If he uses the available documents (authoritative orders, laws) he may get no closer to the examination of the phenomenon, while if he wants to know more about the real nature of indoctrination he must wander off the philosophical paths and get lost on the moors of relativistic and descriptive sociology.

Setting the human software to another program while retaining compatibility with other systems for gaining further information means that indoctrination is in fact an indirect manipulation of thinking. Because of its indirect nature the criteria of irrationality, intention and so on are inappropriate as a definition. The idea of indoctrination as the deviation of our moral compass is beautifully explained in the words of Thorstein Veblen, who in 1915 described militarism as follows:

> It reaches its best efficiency in either case, in war or peace, only when the habit of arbitrary authority and unquestioning obedience has been so thoroughly ingrained that subservience has become a passionate aspiration with the subject population, where the habit of allegiance has attained that degree of automatism that the subject's ideal of liberty has come to be permission to obey orders—somewhat after the fashion in which theologians interpret the freedom of the faithful, whose supreme privilege it is to fulfil all the divine commands.
> (1954, p. 82)

Veblen wrote about the habit of obeying authority and of not questioning things. Formulating this habit leads to the unique perception of freedom—where freedom is to contribute to the general good by fulfilling authoritative (divine, party, scientifically designed and so on) commands. In one respect we might say that indoctrination is the re-examination of the concept of freedom and by the standards of this re-evaluated concept indoctrination would not qualify as indoctrination at all. The elusive nature of the framework of reference makes it difficult to see from the inside whether I am being indoctrinated or not. Whether indoctrination can be detected by its victims is a serious question to be researched.

When obedience through indoctrination becomes a 'habit', part and parcel of everyday life, freedom might appear as an attack on one's integrity. A typical case was the introduction of the 1985 Education Act, which provided teachers in Hungary with significantly greater freedom than they had ever previously had. This partial independence from central authorities was still far from the liberties given by the British system but in relative terms it meant a great shift for Hungarian educators. The first reactions to the increase in freedom were very hostile; teachers in fact experienced the feeling of freedom as a threat. Letters from teachers appeared in the educational press demanding close control and accusing the government of abandoning them. The withdrawal symptom of taking away authority was a cry for authority. Teachers separated the traits of authority from authority itself; they hated what they experienced, not the cause of it. This misconception was in its origin very similar to that of renegade Marxists: the theory is good, only the practice is spoiled. Educators also lived through an existential crisis, for until the Act they could defend themselves with the argument that they were forced to teach what and how they were teaching. Now this shield has been taken away. The general reaction, in my experience, was that *teachers kept on behaving as if they were strictly controlled*. The

1985 Act changed the status of inspectors into that of advisers. This was more than just a change of name; advisers have no authority to control teachers and may visit schools and classrooms only if they are invited or allowed by teachers. In reality both advisers and teachers continued to act as they had done before the Act. Keeping this authoritative role was in the interest of both the ruler and the ruled. One could say that mutually accepted professional control would be an ideal set-up, having nothing to do with indoctrinated teachers. But this is not the case: teachers still, five years after the Act, complain about and suffer from underqualified and arbitrary adviser-inspectors. The situation is taken for granted and has been ingrained in the culture in the same way as the rule that we do not go out in the street naked. The question is obviously not whether we need inspectors or not—this is a partly political and partly professional consideration. The big problem is that either the question does not arise or if it does teachers hardly believe that there could be at least two answers.

If we accept Veblen's approach and see indoctrination as a cultural phenomenon we might be left with the uneasy feeling of fear of a lethal virus that could attack any time, anywhere, and that we might not recognize the epidemic until it was too late. This conclusion would not be very constructive, as was well demonstrated in the 1950s during the McCarthy era in the United States or under the petty dictators in Eastern Europe. Such paranoia would not result in less indoctrination and more freedom, for if we accept that indoctrination is making the range of unquestioned things grow and that the range of free choices will decrease in the same ratio, then it is clear that it is only indoctrination, and not freedom, that could be defended by resistance to alien ideas. Difference frames of reference and means of thinking challenge our cultural paradigms because they throw light on neglected problems or present them from different perspectives. This challenge decreases the number of 'taken-for-granted' values, attitudes or habits in the Veblenian sense, and thus threatens the very nature of indoctrination. All this means that possibly the only weapon against indoctrination could be international, or rather intercultural, exchange.

REFERENCES

Davidov, J. (1965) *Munka es szabadsag* (Work and Freedom). Budapest: Kossuth.
Engels, F. (1975) *A szocializmus fejlodese az utopiatol a tudomanyig* (The Development of Socialism from Utopia to Science). Budapest: Kossuth.
Fichte, J. G. (1968) *Addresses to the German Nation*. New York–Evanston: Harper & Row.
Marx, K. (1960) *Feuerbach tézisck* (Thesis on Feuerbach). In K. Marx and F. Engels, *Collected Works*, Vol. II. Budapest: Kossuth.
Veblen, T. (1954) *Imperial Germany and the Industrial Revolution*. New York: Viking Press.

Chapter 6

Discipline, Internalization and Freedom: A Conceptual Analysis

Jan Steutel

DISCIPLINE: ANALYSIS AND FORMULATION OF THE PROBLEM

Results of empirical research indicate a remarkable change in early parent–child interactions (see Hoffman, 1975, pp. 231, 236–7; 1977, pp. 87–8; 1983, pp. 245–6). During the first year of infancy, parents are mainly acting as persons who offer care and support. Their interactions with the child are dominated by activities like feeding and changing, cuddling and hugging, comforting and helping, protecting and guarding, playing and having fun. In performing these activities, parents have the intention of *gratifying* the wants and needs of the infant. They are trying to optimize his immediate well-being or happiness.

In the course of the second year of childhood, however, a qualitatively different role comes into prominence. More and more parents act as persons who are disciplining and socializing. Activities like prescribing and forbidding, warning and reprimanding, threatening and punishing, urging and exhorting, making demands and giving orders, become prevalent. In contrast to caring and supporting, these activities are characterized by the intention of *frustrating* certain wants and needs of the child. The immediate well-being or happiness of the child is not the focus of attention, but the adaptation of his behaviour to the normative orientation of his parents.

As is well-known, such discipline encounters constitute an important area of social learning theories and (neo-) psychoanalytic research.[1] In both traditions much attention is paid to the effects of different disciplinary techniques on the moral development of the child (cf. for example Hoffman, 1977, pp. 88–96; Cass, 1983; Herbert, 1989). And in both traditions the term 'discipline' (used as a verb) has roughly the following descriptive meaning.

Firstly, the one who disciplines (e.g. the parent) is of the opinion that the one who is disciplined (e.g. the child) is not behaving according to certain rules (norms, standards, criteria, principles). The parent thinks that the child is doing something that should not be done, or that the child is not doing something that should be done. Subsequently, discipline encounters are accompanied by a negative evaluation of (an aspect of) the behaviour of the child, with an element of parental disapproval.

Secondly, the person who disciplines (e.g. the parent) tries to correct the behaviour of the one who is disciplined (e.g. the child). The parent stimulates the child either to desist from the things he does, or to do the things he is refraining from. That is why discipline encounters produce a certain degree of frustration. The child has a want or an inclination to do what is prohibited by the parent. The things that attract him are not allowed. Or the child has an aversion or a disinclination towards behaviour that is ordered by the parent. The things that repel him are imposed.

Thirdly, the aim of the person who disciplines (e.g. the parent) is that the one who is disciplined (e.g. the child) should internalize the relevant rules. In using techniques of discipline, the parent is trying to do more than merely adapt the behaviour of the child to her rules. Above all she is eager to foster learning processes in which the child really makes these rules his own. The normative beliefs of the parent must become part of the child's internal motivational system.

From now on I will use the term 'discipline' according to this definition.[2]

Discipline is a subject of persistent controversy in educational circles. Some people are definite opponents of disciplining the child, in particular the exponents of the so-called *romantic* tradition. A. S. Neill is a striking example of this movement. With the help of an amalgam of psychological and moral arguments, he frankly rejects all processes of discipline. 'I believe,' he writes in his widely read book about Summerhill, 'that to impose anything by authority is wrong' (1960, p. 114). Instead of disciplining, training or moulding the child according to adult conceptions, he must be left free to live his own life, to live in line with his inner nature. Only then will he grow into a person who is happy, mentally sound, creative, original, well balanced, self-confident, sincere, social, friendly and altruistic. In Neill's opinion it is a delusion to think that moral discipline contributes to this development. On the contrary, 'it is moral instruction that makes the child bad' (1960, p. 250).

Others, however, attach great value to discipline. In particular, representatives of the so-called *geisteswissenschaftliche Pädagogik* argue strongly in favour of binding the child to an ideal normative order (Hintjes, 1981, pp. 138–43). A remarkable proponent of this tradition is M. J. Langeveld, a well-known Dutch philosopher of education. In his principal work he observes 'an essential connection between education and authority' (1971, p. 42). In exercising authority, including disciplinary practices, the child is turned towards a moral order, towards moral standards and values which the educator considers obligatory. Only by exerting such an influence will the child develop into an adult; that is, into a person who is characterized by moral responsibility and moral self-determination. According to Langeveld, the belief that this kind of development is possible without exercising authority is a heresy. The reverse is true: 'The child, left to his own devices, . . . would end up in chaos, disorder, arbitrariness, that is: persist in mere vital vegetating' (1971, p. 52).

Perhaps the most striking thing about this controversy is the clash of opinions on the relationship between discipline and *freedom*. In disputing the value of disciplining children, frequent use is made of the persuasive force of terms such as 'freedom' and 'constraint', 'self-government' and 'coercion'. Opponents of discipline usually point to a *negative* relation with freedom. Neill, for example, contrasts the disciplined child with the free one, which he sometimes calls 'the self-regulated child' (1960, pp. 104 ff.). Advocates of discipline, on the other hand, commonly sketch a *positive* relation with freedom. Langeveld, for instance, denies that freedom and authority are at odds. On the contrary, freedom is established by education: 'here authority *creates* freedom' (1971, p. 52).

Now, what position do we have to take *vis-à-vis* these seemingly opposite views? Is the claim that there is a negative relation between discipline and freedom warranted? Or is the contention that a positive relation obtains more tenable? Or are perhaps both views justified? Or is it even possible that neither relation can be demonstrated? Answering these intriguing questions will be the main purpose of this chapter. But it is important immediately to highlight two qualifications.

In the first place I am only interested in relations between the *concepts* of discipline and freedom. The relations I want to trace are no contingent correlations between variables, but logical connections between concepts. In other words, the character of my enquiry is not empirical but philosophical.

In the second place I shall confine my analysis to *moral* discipline. As already stated, disciplinary practices imply the intention of imparting certain rules to the child. These rules are not necessarily moral ones (for example, 'take equal shares!'), but can also be of a different kind, for instance rules of etiquette ('eat with knife and fork!'), rules of prudence ('brush your teeth before going to bed!') or traffic rules ('indicate the direction before making a turn!'). My analysis, however, is only concerned with discipline encounters in which the internalization of moral rules is pursued. As such the subject matter of my enquiry belongs to the domain of moral education.

Given these methodological and thematic restrictions, I will proceed as follows. In the next section the concept of moral internalization is clarified. If moral discipline is directed towards the internalization of moral rules, how then has this aim to be explained? An adequate answer to this question is a prerequisite for grasping the conceptual relations between moral discipline and freedom. The final section attempts to reveal some of these connections. By distinguishing three concepts of freedom, different relations with discipline are mapped.

INTERNALIZATION: SEARCHING FOR AN ADEQUATE ANALYSIS

Sometimes 'internalization' is used as a *process* word: it refers to some sort of learning process, to the way in which the child makes certain rules his own. At other times, however, 'internalization' is used as a *product* word: it relates to the results of those learning processes, to the fact that the child has made certain rules his own. In this section I will try to clarify the product use of the word: what do we mean when we say that someone has internalized a moral rule?

A first answer to this question is given in terms of *objective* or *external* criteria, in particular within the framework of experimental research into the relations between discipline and internalization (see, for example, Aronfreed, 1968a). In performing these experiments, first of all the child is subjected to different disciplinary techniques. Then it is determined whether or not these techniques have led to internalized regulation. For that purpose the child is placed in a situation in which (i) certain temptations are present, (ii) surveillance of adults is absent, and (iii) sanctions like punishment and reward are excluded. When the child is behaving well under these conditions, it is assumed that internalized regulation has been induced.

As part of experimental research, such an operational definition may be useful. But it is not an adequate explanation of the concept of internalization. At the very most the listed criteria are necessary conditions for the applicability of 'internalization'. It may be true that a person who has internalized certain rules normally observes those rules in the specified circumstances. But together the criteria are certainly *not* sufficient. Suppose that the child, despite the factual absence of possible sanctions, is still motivated by the image of a punishing father. Or that the child, even if external control is excluded, nevertheless is guided by the sense of a vindictive, omnipresent authority (cf. Aronfreed and Reber, 1965, pp. 3–4; Aronfreed, 1968b, p. 35; Hoffman, 1970, p. 263; 1977, pp. 123–4). If these motives are strong enough, the child will keep the rules in the specified situation. But because he is merely moved by (albeit groundless) fear of punishment or requital, the claim that he has internalized these rules is untenable.

These counter-examples show that an external definition fails to discriminate between pure conformism and internalization. In cases of pure conformism, compliance with rules is produced only by *extrinsic* motives, such as avoiding condemnation and ridicule, acquiring reward and approval, yielding to social pressure, upholding one's good reputation, delighting authorities, gaining pecuniary advantage, fear of losing one's job, or concern for the opinion of one's neighbours. For such a person acting according to rules has merely instrumental value: he complies with the rules in order to obtain personal advantage. Conformism that results only from extrinsic motives indicates the absence of internalized rules. And the trouble with an external definition is that such kinds of motivation are not excluded.[3]

A second answer refers to certain *subjective* or *internal* criteria, namely, to *intrinsic* desires (or inclinations) and aversions (or disinclinations) (see, for example Brandt, 1979, pp. 165–6, 287). The internalization of moral rules (such as the obligation to fulfil one's promises) implies *ipso facto* the acquisition of desires and aversions towards behaviour or states of affairs to which these rules apply (for example the desire to redeem one's promises, or an aversion to breaking one's promises). And these desires and aversions are intrinsic by nature, which means 'not *derivative*, or at least *not wholly* derivative, from some other want/aversion' (Brandt, 1970, p. 30; cf. pp. 33–4).

This explanation of 'internalization' circumvents the difficulties of the external definition discussed earlier. By highlighting intrinsic motives, conformism due to mere extrinsic incentives is ruled out. Nevertheless the proposed internal criteria are not sufficient. These criteria, too, only refer to necessary conditions for the proper use of 'internalization'. A person who has internalized moral rules is indeed normally moved by correlating intrinsic desires and aversions. But merely being motivated like this is not a sufficient condition of moral internalization.

Suppose that a person is characterized by sympathy and care for his fellow-man. Such feelings involve intrinsic desires and aversions, including the desire to help people in distress. Can we conclude from this that the person in question has internalized the moral prescription to render assistance to people in distress? Not right away. For if his aid to people is *only* motivated by feelings of sympathy and care, he is indifferent to the *moral quality* of his behaviour (Herman, 1981, pp. 365–6). His motives may be very charming, but what is missing is the motivational notion that offering help in the specified circumstances is *morally required*. It is true that he acts in accordance with the rule; but he is not moved *by* the rule. He has an intrinsic desire to perform actions that are morally required; but he does not act *from* the consideration that his actions meet this moral qualification. And is that not exactly what we expect from someone who has internalized moral rules?

A third answer also calls attention to subjective or internal criteria; this time, however, not to intrinsic desires and aversions, but to a qualitatively different kind of intrinsic motivation: a *sense of duty* (Hoffman, 1983, pp. 243–4). In my opinion, this explanation of 'internalization' is defensible, provided that 'a sense of duty' is interpreted as follows.

First, the sense of duty of a person who has internalized moral rules has to be construed broadly. A sense of duty is usually conceived as an internal correlate of moral rules that lay down which behaviour is, in certain circumstances, morally *required* (so-called duties and obligations). Sometimes, however, a sense of duty is in addition conceived as a subjective correlate of moral rules that indicate which behaviour is, in certain situations, morally *recommendable* (so-called rules of supererogation). According to this view, a sense of duty encompasses *both* the motivating consideration that particular behaviour is morally required and the motivating consideration that certain behaviour is morally recommendable (cf. Baron, 1984, p. 201). And because processes of internalization involve both types of moral rules, it is advisable to observe this broad use of 'a sense of duty'.

Secondly, a sense of duty as a result of successful internalization implies the conviction that the correlating moral rules are *valid* or *justified*. Take, for instance, the moral obligation to return borrowed goods in due course. Effective internalization of this rule will result in acting from a sense of duty, in this case from the consideration that bringing back borrowed goods on time is morally required. And this acquired sense of duty implies the conviction that the indicated rule is valid, or at least the conviction that there are good reasons for believing in the validity of this rule. Indeed, being moved by a sense of duty, or being moved by one's own conviction that the corresponding moral rules are valid or justified, amount to the same thing.

Thirdly, the sense of duty of the one who has internalized moral rules operates normally as a *secondary* motive (cf. Baron, 1984, p. 207). A sense of duty that functions as a primary motive can, by itself, produce action. As a secondary motive, however, a sense of duty is not sufficient to bring about action. Without the *support* of desires or aversions that point in the same direction it cannot prompt one to act. Nonetheless, a sense of duty that operates as a secondary motive is really a motive. For only by virtue of the *sanctioning* by a secondary sense of duty will the desires or aversions result in action. Suppose, for example, that a person has internalized the moral prohibition not to steal. On the one hand, his aversion to theft will give motivational support to his conviction that refraining from stealing is morally required. His intrinsic aversion sustains his sense of duty. On the other hand, his conviction that abstaining from stealing is morally required will tell him that he has to honour his aversion to theft. His sense of duty approves his compliance with his intrinsic aversion.

FREEDOM: ANALYSIS OF RELATIONS WITH DISCIPLINE

Moral discipline exerts a correcting influence with the intention of fostering the internalization of moral rules. And moral internalization consists in the establishment of a subtle interplay between a sense of duty and intrinsic desires and aversions (Duff, 1980, pp. 230–1). This is, in a nutshell, the outcome of our analysis. Can we now, on the basis of this analysis, trace some conceptual relations between moral discipline and freedom? Is it logically possible to describe the *intended* effect of moral discipline in terms of freedom?

It is, I think, undeniable that a *negative* or *exclusive* connection between discipline and freedom obtains. In the first section of this chapter I presented an analysis of 'discipline'. The second defining condition concerned the correcting interference of the parent. The child is encouraged to abstain from the things he finds attractive, or to do the things he finds repugnant. The aim of the parent is to motivate the child to behave contrary to his desires or aversions. As such the intended effect of discipline is decidedly a curtailment of the freedom of the child.

But what do we mean by 'freedom' in this context? Which particular concept of freedom is being applied? To put it briefly: here the word 'freedom' is used to refer to creatures that are in no way impeded in following their desires and aversions. This concept of freedom I shall call *animal* freedom.[4] A child who is free, in this sense of the word, can do as he pleases. He is not obstructed by anything or anyone in doing the things to which he is attracted, or in omitting the things by which he is repelled. And it is exactly this animal freedom which is restricted by discipline. For discipline is *ipso facto* an attempt to prevent the child from practising certain inclinations or disinclinations.

Most of us will know from childhood experience this negative relation between discipline and freedom. I myself was born and bred in the so-called neo-Calvinistic or New Reformed sociopolitical tradition. This subculture was characterized by striking religious–moral beliefs concerning subjects like authority and obedience, domesticity and sexuality, labour, art and play, the man–woman relationship, and the keeping of the Sabbath (see Sturm, 1988). With regard to the last of these, there was an explicit prohibition against swimming on Sunday, even if the weather was hot and going to the beach was tempting, and a duty to attend the Sunday sermons, even though these sermons were long-winded and boring. When we made preparations to do things that we found attractive (swimming on Sunday), this was disallowed; and when we tried to duck out of doing things that we thought tedious (attending endless sermons), this was demanded. During such discipline encounters we felt literally unfree, in the animal sense of the word.

So Neill is, in a certain respect, quite right in suggesting that discipline and freedom are opposites. Nevertheless there is something curious about his line of thought. In his book on Summerhill he argues strongly in favour of the free child and repeatedly rejects *all* disciplinary practices (see for example Neill, 1960, pp. 4, 113, 254). But other parts of the same book clearly indicate that the freedom of Summerhill children is curtailed by a web of rules. Not only rules of prudence are imposed, such as the prohibition against climbing on the roof or cycling on the street alone (pp. 20–1). All sorts of moral rules, which actually specify the principle of respect for the freedom of others, obtain as well (pp. 114, 155, 348). And if the members of Summerhill violate these rules, then discipline, including punishment, is not eschewed: 'The community has the right to restrain the antisocial boy because he is interfering with the rights of others' (1960, p. 115; cf. pp. 50–1, 155, 157).

But why this correcting way of action? Surely to induce an intrinsic commitment to a certain moral orientation? And is that not an attempt to make *another* kind of freedom possible?

Indeed, we can also point to a *positive* or *inclusive* connection between discipline and freedom. In order to reveal this relation it is important to recall the third defining condition of 'discipline': the intention of fostering the internalization of rules. And the aim of moral discipline, I argued, is the internalization of moral rules. Given our explanation of 'internalization', pursuing this aim consists in teaching the child to take command of his life by observing moral rules of his own accord. In other words, the target of moral discipline is that the child develops from a creature that is governed by his desires and aversions into a person that governs *himself* by attuning his doings and dealings to self-accepted moral rules. As such the intended effect of moral discipline is the advancement of freedom in the sense of self-determination or self-regulation.

It may be clear that this type of freedom is not the same as animal freedom. What is the content of this alternative concept of freedom? Roughly formulated this concept is applicable to people who order their lives independently according to a self-accepted normative orientation. This kind of freedom I shall call *autarchic* freedom.[5] A person who is free in this sense of the word is motivated by a conception of life to which he gives his own assent, by an authentic view concerning the arrangement of his life. Moreover, he is capable of practising his normative orientation, with the result that his life shows a certain structure and coherence.

Moral discipline is finally meant to make this freedom possible. By fostering the internalization of moral rules, building blocks are supplied for the establishment of a *moral* conception of life. The aim is to contribute to the development of *moral* autarchic freedom. A person who is free in this respect is motivated by a sense of duty. Since a sense of duty implies the conviction that the correlating moral rules are valid or justified, this person is moved by an authentic conception, by a moral orientation which has his own consent.[6] In addition to this, the person has the capacity to put his sense of duty into action. He himself is able to order his life according to his moral conception. Such a person is not determined by the strength of attraction and repulsion, but determines his life himself on the basis of a moral orientation which is really his own (see Baron, 1985, p. 147).

The typical exponents of the neo-Calvinistic subculture were such autarchic persons. They felt it their duty to make, if possible, a good marriage, to start a family, and to raise their children according to the reformational doctrine; they counted it their duty to practise a decent profession, in a diligent and persevering manner; they thought it their duty to be loyal members of the Reformed church; and especially they were persuaded of the duty to keep the Ten Commandments. In short, they subscribed to a particular religious–moral orientation, defined their long-term objectives within that framework, and ordered their lives accordingly. And their disciplinary practices were not primarily intended to frustrate the desires and aversions of their children, but above all to bind their offspring to this orientation in order that the same inner compass would set the course of their lives too.

So Langeveld is also right when he draws attention to a positive connection between exercising authority and freedom. This freedom, which is characteristic of the adult, is nothing other than knowing values and norms, and being disposed to live accordingly.

Human freedom, Langeveld writes, *is* restraint, namely, being bound by a moral order with which one identifies oneself. Therefore adulthood reveals itself as *form*. By virtue of his commitment to a moral orientation, the life of the adult shows plan, line and objective, the opposite of chaos, disorder and arbitrariness (Langeveld, 1971, pp. 45, 52).

But, one might ask, is it not suggested that the life of the moral autarchic person is unpleasant and joyless as well? All this talking about duty and bondage, does that not evoke the image of a life without spontaneity and full of painful effort? And is that image not confirmed by the example of the neo-Calvinists? In my opinion, this impression is, broadly speaking, mistaken. For it should be remembered that the sense of duty of the one who has internalized moral rules usually operates as a *secondary* motive. In general his sense of duty is supported by congenial desires and aversions. He normally enjoys the things he does from duty, and dislikes the things he forbears from duty. The leading lights of the neo-Calvinistic movement attached great importance to this concordance of duty and inclination. Witness for example the words of the new Reformed Dutch ethicist G. Brillenburg Wurth: 'It is not true, that "duty" and "inclination" are destined, in a Kantian vein, to be two and to remain two. Duty has to become our inclination. It must come to this . . . that we take "delight in the law of God after the inward man" (Rom. VII. 22), that we experience something of "the Rejoicing of the Law", that "our heart is inclined unto God's testimonies" (Psalm CXIX. 36)' (1958, p. 85; cf. Sturm, 1984, pp. 152–3).

So moral discipline involves the intention of fostering autarchic freedom by restricting animal freedom. Simultaneously with the establishment of a sense of duty, the development of congenial intrinsic desires and aversions is pursued. And in so far as this harmony of duty and (dis)inclination finally takes shape, the person who is free in the autarchic sense of the word is also free in the animal sense.[7]

In the literature on moral education yet another ideal of freedom is recommended. This ideal is known as *moral autonomy* (cf. for example Hare, 1975; Peters, 1981, pp. 120–2, 152–5). Is it perhaps possible to trace some logical connections between our concept of discipline and this concept of freedom too? In order to answer this question, first of all the descriptive meaning of 'moral autonomy' has to be explained. What is the content of this concept of freedom?

The morally autonomous person has, I think, all the positive characteristics of autarchy. He, too, orders his life independently according to a moral orientation which he has accepted for himself. But in addition to that, he is the bearer of qualities which are not implied in autarchic freedom, in particular the ability and tendency to think *critically* about the validity of moral rules. On the one hand, the autonomous person has the *ability* to subject moral rules to a process of rational assessment. He is capable of evaluating moral rules in the light of procedural principles, including the principle of impartiality and the principle of the consideration of interests. These principles define what counts as a relevant argument in a rational discourse about moral problems. As such they are constitutive of critical moral reasoning (Steutel, 1989a, pp. 109–12). What is more, the morally autonomous person has, when appropriate, a *tendency* to reflect critically upon moral rules. This disposition shows itself for example when he is confronted with new moral problems that arise from developments in science and technology; or when his moral rules conflict by accident and it is not intuitively clear which rule is of overriding importance; or when his moral rules conflict by necessity with the rules of others, which is not unusual in a pluralistic society (Steutel, 1989b, pp. 61–3).

In other words, the essential difference between autarchy and autonomy is located in the ability and tendency to think critically about the validity of moral rules. The autarchic person, to be sure, is convinced that his moral rules are valid or justified. But it is not at all necessary that he is able or disposed to put forward a rational justification of these rules.[8] The neo-Calvinists, for instance, did not ground their religious–moral rules in their own reason (autonomy), but in the commanding will of the external Lawgiver (theonomy). They were convinced of the validity of their moral law because they regarded it as part of God's Revelation (Sturm, 1988, pp. 109–14). And what about the so-called traditionalists? They have faith not in the power of individual reason but in the hidden value and wisdom of traditions. To them, the fact that a moral rule is part of tradition is in itself a good reason to comply with it (Cooper, 1970, pp. 84–5).

Now, what is the relation between moral discipline and autonomous freedom? To my mind this connection is *neutral*, that is to say neither negative or exclusive, nor positive or inclusive. On the one hand, a *negative* relation between discipline and autonomy is absent. Moral discipline is not necessarily intended to discourage the development of critical qualities. Some disciplinary techniques can even be applied with a view to contributing actively to this development. Inductive discipline, for example, in which the child's attention is drawn to the adverse effects of his behaviour on the welfare of others, is a form of exerting a rational influence. By disciplining the child in this way, the insight can be induced that certain rules are founded in the procedural principle of the consideration of interests (cf. Peters, 1981, p. 154; Hoffman, 1987, p. 60 ff.). Even if one is convinced that the child is not yet able to understand an autonomous principled justification, discipline can be exercised within a framework of asking and giving reasons in the hope that the child, as time goes by, will be able and disposed to subject his moral rules to a critical examination (see Van Haaften, 1988, pp. 34–7).

On the other hand, neither does a *positive* connection between discipline and autonomy obtain. Moral discipline is not necessarily intended to encourage the development of critical qualities either. It is by no means impossible that disciplinary practices may be accompanied by the intention of obstructing this development. New Reformed authorities, for instance, have repeatedly alerted the young generation to the dangers of an independent critical examination of their own religious-moral beliefs (Sturm, 1988, p. 134). Certainly, in disciplining the young they were striving for the establishment of a sense of duty, and thus of the conviction that the Reformed orientation is valid or justified. But at the same time they intended to avert critical reflection concerning the very same beliefs.

This neutral connection between discipline and autonomy can also be described in terms of *indoctrination*. Let us, with Spiecker (see Chapter 2), accept that indoctrination consists in deliberately thwarting the development of critical qualities, of intellectual virtues and rational emotions. Since ways of disciplining are not logically connected with this intention, moral discipline is not *ipso facto* indoctrination. We can discipline our children without indoctrinating them. But because processes of discipline are also not necessarily accompanied by the intention of fostering the growth of intellectual virtues and rational emotions, moral discipline can be *de facto* indoctrination. We can indoctrinate our children by disciplining them.

NOTES

(1)   In classical psychoanalysis, processes of discipline are connected with the Oedipal phase, which is located between the fourth and the sixth year of childhood. In neo-psychoanalytic research, however, great importance is attached to disciplinary practices in the preceding period, which begins at the end of the first year of infancy (see, for example, Emde *et al.*, 1987, pp. 258, 270).

(2)   Often the term 'discipline' is used (or explained) differently. Some people use (or consider) the word 'discipline' as synonymous with 'punishment'. But if we observe my definition, punishment is just one of many disciplinary techniques. Others use (or conceive) 'discipline' as a word that denotes all forms of 'submission to rules that structure what has to be learnt' (Hirst and Peters, 1970, p. 125; cf. Peters, 1966, p. 267). According to my definition, however, the word 'discipline' is only applicable to certain practices the object of which is 'submission to rules'.

(3)   According to J. Aronfreed, 'internalized behavioral suppression' can be produced by means of processes of conditioning in which (i) anxiety is attached directly to intrinsic correlates of undesirable behaviour (for example cognitive representations of that behaviour) and (ii) anxiety reduction is attached directly to intrinsic correlates of desirable behavioural alternatives (cf. Aronfreed and Reber, 1965, pp. 4–5; Aronfreed, 1968a, pp. 286–7). It may be true that a child who is acting from such intrinsic correlates meets the criteria of the external definition. But because the child is acting rightly only in order to reduce conditioned anxiety, the assumption that he has internalized some rule is not warranted. Because the desirable behaviour has merely 'instrumental value' to the child (anxiety reduction), he is only extrinsically motivated.

(4)   The adjective 'animal' is used because animals, too, can be free or unfree in the sense explained. At least some animals have wants and aversions, and can be hindered in following them. Witness, for example, the training of dogs, which can be regarded as a certain form of discipline. But because acting from duty is typical of human beings only, animals cannot be subjected to *moral* discipline.

(5)   I have taken the word 'autarchy' from the work of S. I. Benn (1988, pp. 154–5, 163–4). In his opinion, the autarchic agent has the capacity to order his life according to a *nomos*. But it is possible that this capacity may not be exercised, or does not attain its full development, as a consequence of which the autarchic person is in fact *anomic*, acting on impulse and on whim (cf. pp. 164, 176). According to my explanation, however, autarchic freedom is inextricably bound up with having *nomoi*. In other words, someone who is in my view autarchic is, in the words of Benn, a *nomic* autarchic person. For such a person he sometimes reserves the term 'self-determining' or 'self-governing' (1988, pp. 192–3).

(6)   Having an authentic commitment to moral rules is *not* logically connected with having adopted them by means of critical reflection. Being moved by the conviction that one's rules are valid or justified is in itself a sufficient condition of an authentic commitment; someone who is motivated like that gives his own assent to those rules. But the indicated conviction does not necessarily imply that one has some idea of the reasons that sustain one's rules, let alone that one is able and disposed to articulate the sort of thing that would constitute a rational appraisal (see Brandt, 1979, p. 169).

(7)   It is, of course, not impossible that the sense of duty of the autarchic person may come into conflict with strong counter-inclinations. In such cases he will try to exercise self-control. Motivated by a primary sense of duty, he will try to discipline *himself* and to make *himself* unfree, in the animal sense of that word.

(8)   In some respects the autarchic person is autonomous as well: he has a moral orientation (*nomos*) to which he gives his own (*autos*) assent. But unlike the autonomous person, he does not necessarily have the equipment to think for himself (*autos*) about moral

rules in accordance with a set of procedural principles (*nomos*). Therefore we could perhaps typify autarchic freedom as *minimal* autonomy, and autonomous freedom as *maximal* autonomy.

REFERENCES

Aronfreed, J. (1968a) Aversive control of socialization. In W. J. Arnold (ed.) *Nebraska Symposium on Motivation*, Vol. XVI. Lincoln: University of Nebraska Press.

Aronfreed, J. (1968b) *Conduct and Conscience. The Socialization of Internalized Control over Behavior*. New York: Academic Press.

Aronfreed, J. and Reber, R. (1965) Internalized behavioral suppression and the timing of social punishment. *Journal of Personality and Social Psychology*, **1**, 3–16.

Baron, M. (1984) The alleged moral repugnance of acting from duty. *The Journal of Philosophy*, **81**, 197–220.

Baron, M. (1985) The ethics of duty/ethics of virtue debate and its relevance to educational theory. *Educational Theory*, **35**, 135–49.

Benn, S. I. (1988) *A Theory of Freedom*. Cambridge: Cambridge University Press.

Brandt, R. B. (1970) Traits of character: a conceptual analysis. *American Philosophical Quarterly*, **7**, 23–37.

Brandt, R. B. (1979) *A Theory of the Good and the Right*. Oxford: Clarendon Press.

Brillenburg Wurth, G. (1958) *Eerherstel van de deugd*. Kampen: Kok.

Cass, L. K. (1983) Discipline from the psychoanalytic viewpoint. In D. Dorr, M. Zax and J. W. Bonner (eds) *The Psychology of Discipline*. New York: International Universities Press.

Cooper, N. (1970) Two concepts of morality. In G. Wallace and A. D. M. Walker (eds) *The Definition of Morality*. London: Methuen.

Duff, A. (1980) Desire, duty and moral absolutes. *Philosophy*, **55**, 223–38.

Emde, R. N., Johnson, W. F. and Easterbrooks, M. A. (1987) The dos and don'ts of early moral development: psychoanalytic tradition and current research. In J. Kagan and S. Lamb (eds) *The Emergence of Morality in Young Children*. Chicago: University of Chicago Press.

Hare, R. M. (1975) Chairman's remarks. In S. C. Brown (ed.) *Philosophers Discuss Education*. London: Macmillan.

Herbert, M. (1989) *Discipline. A Positive Guide for Parents*. Oxford: Basil Blackwell.

Herman, B. (1981) On the value of acting from the motive of duty. *The Philosophical Review*, **90**, 359–82.

Hintjes, J. (1981) *Geesteswetenschappelijke pedagogiek*. Meppel: Boom.

Hirst, P. H. and Peters, R. S. (1970) *The Logic of Education*. London: Routledge & Kegan Paul.

Hoffman, M. L. (1970) Moral development. In P. H. Mussen (ed.) *Carmichael's Manual of Child Psychology*, Vol. II. New York: John Wiley & Sons.

Hoffman, M. L. (1975) Moral internalization, parental power, and the nature of parent–child interaction. *Developmental Psychology*, **11**, 228–39.

Hoffman, M. L. (1977) Moral internalization: current theory and research. In L. Berkowitz (ed.) *Advances in Experimental Social Psychology*. New York: Academic Press.

Hoffman, M. L. (1983) Affective and cognitive processes in moral internalization. In E. T. Higgins, D. N. Ruble and W. W. Hartup (eds) *Social Cognition and Social Development. A Sociocultural Perspective*. Cambridge: Cambridge University Press.

Hoffman, M. L. (1987) The contribution of empathy to justice and moral judgment. In N. Eisenberg and J. Strayer (eds) *Empathy and Its Development*. Cambridge: Cambridge University Press.

Langeveld, M. J. (1971) *Beknopte theoretische pedagogiek*. Groningen: Wolters-Noordhoff.

Neill, A. S. (1960) *Summerhill: A Radical Approach to Child Rearing* (1926). New York: Hart Publishing Company.

Peters, R. S. (1966) *Ethics and Education*. London: Allen & Unwin.

Peters, R. S. (1981) *Moral Development and Moral Education*. London: Allen & Unwin.

Steutel, J. W. (1989a) Over morele en intellectuele deugden. *Pedagogische Studiën*, **66**, 107–18.

Steutel, J. W. (1989b) Twee centrale doelen van de morele opvoeding. *Pedagogisch Tijdschrift*, special edition, 61–6.

Sturm, J. C. (1984) Gereformeerde opvattingen over zedelijke opvoeding: 'de wet, dat is de liefde'. In J. W. Steutel (ed.) *Morele opvoeding. Theoretisch- en historisch- pedagogische opstellen*. Meppel: Boom.

Sturm, J. C. (1988) *Een goede gereformeerde opvoeding. Over neo-calvinistische moraal-pedagogiek (1880–1950), met speciale aandacht voor de nieuw-gereformeerde jeugdorga-nisaties*. Kampen: Kok.

Van Haaften, A. W. (1988) Can moral education be justified in moral education? In B. Spiecker and R. Straughan (eds) *Philosophical Issues in Moral Education and Development*. Milton Keynes: Open University Press.

Chapter 7

Freedom and Learning: Some Thoughts on Liberal and Progressive Education

Jürgen Oelkers

Il n'y a guère qu'une naissance honnête, ou qu'une bonne éducation, qui rendent les hommes capables de secret.
(La Bruyère)

INTRODUCTION

Education and freedom have often been linked together in the context of pedagogical theories but never without contradiction. It was Kant who formulated the most prominent version of this contradiction that turns into a paradox: to educate means to put constraints on the child but only this compulsion will help him to promote his freedom. So the crucial question for every theory of education must be: how can freedom be cultivated if constraints cannot be avoided?[1] For Kant compulsion is a necessary but not a sufficient condition for an education which frees man's mind and cultivates his manners.

Kant's dictum is seen as a kind of scandal for educational theory because the educational public has learned, mainly under the influence of progressive education, that means and ends of education must not be contradictory. On the other hand the child is not born with the ability to make full use of his 'free' mind. He must acquire knowledge and forms of understanding as a sufficient framework for acting. The child is not just 'growing', but is one allowed to *force* the child to learn and to steer him in a defined direction? Must not all learning be free in the sense that the child decides for himself what he wants to learn? If this were true there would be no contradiction between freedom and education, because there would be no education and only learning, but does a child really know what is best for his own learning?

These are not new questions, but they are questions which have remained unanswered. There are two standard dogmas disguised as theories and I find neither of them very helpful in clarifying the concept. According to the first, education is conceived as a means to an end which is itself 'good'; in this case, indoctrination is justified by the *aim* of education. When 'freedom' is the aim of education, even means that put coercion on the child can be applied, provided they lead the process of education to a good end. Those who hold the second dogma view education as support for the natural development of the child, which is what they consider to be the desirable aim. In this case indoctrination is not justified, but neither is education. Promoting natural development means that the child should become committed only to those moral obligations considered 'natural'. On this interpretation education is nothing but indoctrination.

Kant's solution, tolerating the contradiction and working with a theory that remains paradoxical, has never been accepted in the modern history of educational thinking. But do we have alternatives? I will discuss the problem in three stages: first, I will refer to *liberal education*, a concept that was discussed in the eighteenth century and is still a focus of attention today. 'Liberal' does not mean *free*, and liberal education, so it seems, cannot be lured into the trap of Kant's paradox. Secondly, I will analyse the concept of *child-centred education*, progressive education's battle-cry at the turn of the nineteenth century and a metaphor not for 'liberal' but for 'free' education. Thirdly, I will compare these two 'paradigms' and will argue against the second and in favour of the first. Kant's paradox can be solved when we reconstruct liberal education as a process of forming the mind, which is fundamentally a process of *self-forming* that cannot be described by a means-and-end analysis.

LIBERAL EDUCATION

Liberal education is a humanist concept: education is founded in nature but 'nature needs to be assisted' (Bantock, 1980, p. 98). The best aid for human nature is *knowledge*, but knowledge in a liberal form. Knowledge can free the mind only if it promotes liberal thinking which is opposed to dogmatism. So all dogmatic knowledge must be excluded if liberal education is to take place. But can there be any learning without dogmatic knowledge? Teaching must make some use of dogmas even when its aim is liberal thinking. But knowledge cannot be taught without a form, and all forms, not only the scholastic ones, represent dogmas, at least during the time of learning.

In the eyes of Sir Thomas Elyot, writing in 1531, learning is an all-embracing affair; it is not just schooling. It has to do with classical studies but also with practical arts, and Elyot (1962) saw no contradiction between the theoretical and the practical part of learning, because only together can they form the whole man. Unfortunately humanistic concepts do not describe 'real' learning but only its 'ideal' outcome. Human experience has always to do with 'distempers' of learning. Bacon, in his *Advancement of Learning* (1605) listed three of these distempers: men learn 'words and no matter'; they learn only the 'beauty of words' and not the 'substance of matter'; and finally they learn the 'untruth' and 'destroy the essential form of knowledge, which is nothing but representation of truth' (1975, p. 69 ff.). Schooling means in most cases inadequate learning. Schoolmen are teaching words, not matter, and in school children are learning the beauty of words, not the substance of matter. And this has to do with dogmatic knowledge which hinders liberal education: 'Schoolmen', Bacon wrote, have

> sharp and strong wits, an abundance of leisure, and small variety of reading; but their wits being shut up in the cells of a very few authors (chiefly Aristotle their dictator) as their persons were shut up in the cells of monasteries and colleges; and knowing little history,

either of nature or time; did out of no great quantity of matter, and infinite agitation of wit, spin out unto us those laborious webs of learning which are extant in their books. (1975, p. 72)

More than two hundred years later John Stuart Mill, the nineteenth century advocate of liberal education, stated in one of his early essays entitled 'On Genius': 'Modern education is all *cram*—Latin cram, mathematical cram, literary cram, political cram, theological cram, moral cram. The world already knows everything, and has only to tell it to its children, who, on their part, have only to hear, and lay it to the rote (not to the *heart*). Any purpose, any idea of training the mind itself, has gone out of the world' (1965, p. 99). This was written in 1832,[2] yet it seems as if Mill is delivering a modern criticism of educational indoctrination in schools.

The metaphor 'cramming' is still in use and educators regularly discuss topics such as the repressive effects and anti-liberal tendencies of the modern school system, thereby following Mill, who, in *On Liberty*, argued that 'a general state education is a mere contrivance for moulding people to be exactly like one another' (1974, p. 177; cf. Warnock, 1988). But the issue is not just the contradiction between humanistic liberal education and state control over public schools; rather one must ask whether education can avoid indoctrination at all. Education, in the humanistic sense of the word, has to impart knowledge to the pupil,[3] and the pupil can be considered to be free to a moderate extent; but even if the pupil has absolute freedom of choice about what he intends to learn, he is not free to invent all the knowledge that he is to learn. He cannot 'rationally choose' his own curriculum.

Mill criticized 'cramming' as the wrong method of learning. 'Cramming' contradicts the concept of education, because the mind of the child is not regarded as a faculty of *active* powers.[4] Liberal education is not 'committing to memory' the *results* of science and leaving the mind passive (Mill, 1965, p. 100). The concept can be expressed more positively as follows: 'The end of education is not to *teach*, but to fit the mind for learning from its own consciousness and observation . . . we have occasion for this power under ever-varying circumstances, for which no routine or rule of thumb can possibly make provision' (1965, p. 101). Learning is an active power and has to do with the use of the mind; teaching is not just filling the mind with knowledge.

So Mill argued for a concept of education in which means and ends are not contradictory: if the aim of education is to supply the mind with knowledge, and therefore develop the child's understanding, then its means cannot be forms of 'cramming'. The means must serve the aim:

> As the memory is trained by remembering, so is the reasoning power by reasoning; the imaginative by imagining; the analytic by analysing; the inventive by finding out. Let the education of mind consist in calling out and exercising these faculties; never trouble yourself about giving knowledge—train the mind—keep it supplied with materials, and knowledge will come of itself. Let all *cram* be ruthlessly discarded.
> (ibid.)

This is not an argument for progressive education, because Mill does not presume the *natural* development of mind but the self-building of understanding. The mind must be considered free to learn and that means it needs knowledge in which understanding can grow, not as a natural occurrence but as the result of the effort of learning, even in a genius. In 1784, a scant fifty years before Mill's 'On Genius', Vicesimus Knox wrote that industry is necessary for everybody, including the genius (1784, sect. XXIV). What educates is the effort of learning, not just natural genius. The argument is interesting: 'genius' may be just the parents' idle hope, an attribution, not a psychological fact (*ibid.*, p. 220 ff.);[5] but even as a *rare* phenomenon genius needs instruction because no man is 'born with knowledge' and knowledge is needed for all higher learning (*ibid.*, p. 225). Learning is identified with school learning and this is every child's best employment, 'for I am sure, that industry, by presenting a constant succession of various objects, and by precluding the listlessness of inaction, renders life at all stages of it agreeable, and particularly so in the restless season of youth' (*ibid.*).

This seems to be only an argument *pro domo*, the idealization of school learning in the eyes of a schoolteacher; but apart from that the argument leads to a crucial question: if genius is not a sufficient condition for the mind to develop, what else is needed for proper education? Who is organizing the knowledge that cannot be acquired just by intuition (or participation in everyday life)? Can there be 'proper' education without the supposition of a self-learning mind, for example a 'genius'? 'Genius' is here used in its eighteenth-century sense as an aesthetic term describing what the Earl of Shaftesbury called 'inward form' or mind as *inward beauty* (1978, Vol. XI, p. 83 ff.). It is '*Mind* alone which forms. All that is void of Mind is horrid: and Matter formless is *Deformity it-self*' (*ibid.*, p. 405). Man's '*inward constitution*' (*ibid.*, p. 84) is a work of art, an aesthetic '*Order* and *Oeconomy*' (*ibid.*, p. 134), not a product of education. Mind as inward form is creative and whole; teaching would only destroy its beauty.[6]

Many theorists of education in the eighteenth century found this position irresponsible. Their views laid emphasis on religious and moral education, leaving the choice of only two possibilities: the good and the evil (cf. Chapone, 1783). On the other hand the power of education was highly estimated: 'There cannot be a good and wise community, made up of foolish and vicious individuals; and individuals cannot be made wise or good, but by education' (Sheridan, 1769, p. 8). This point seems to be self-evident; the only question is why 'so little attention has been paid to it' (*ibid.*, pp. 14,15). This has to do with the existing system of education which is 'the true source of all our follies, vices, ignorance and false taste' (*ibid.*, pp. 16,17).

Sheridan, like Mill, criticized the manner of instruction and the omission of useful studies in contemporary schools. But Sheridan did not argue for liberal education, because for him the basic principles of all education must be derived from religion (*ibid.*, p. 42).

Liberal education can tolerate religion, but only as a form of knowledge, not as dogma. Religion may supply useful knowledge but cannot define education. Education, as Joseph Priestley wrote in 1778, must be understood as the qualification of men, not as the forming of a dogmatic mind. Liberal education has its own definition:

> The general object of education is evidently to qualify men to appear to advantage in future life, which can only be done by communicating to them such *knowledge*, and leading them to form such *habits*, as will be the most useful to them hereafter: and in this *the whole of their future being*, to which their education can be supposed to bear any relation, is to be considered.
> (Priestley, 1778, p. 9)

Education is *enlightenment* of mind (cf. Williams, 1774),[7] and at the same time the forming of habits. Religion cannot be taught without reason, otherwise 'a mechanical habit will be formed' (Priestley, 1778, p. 83). The idea, contrary to Rousseau, is to form a 'perfect *man*' and a 'perfect *citizen*' without indoctrination (*ibid.*, p. 144). Education is *public* experience and its medium is true knowledge that can be used in practical life (*ibid.*, pp. 185,195).[8] Given this, 'liberal education' (*ibid.*, p. 195) can be neither useless nor coercive, because it improves the mind's understanding and the business of everyday life. Education cannot be indoctrination because it consists in studies that are voluntary and useful for life.

But is education that innocent? David Fordyce discussed liberal education as a dialogue between two options of liberal education that can be called the *Shaftesbury* and the *Priestley* principle of learning.[9] The first principle is opting for genius, the second for organized knowledge, and both can be argued for with good reasons. Fordyce called the protagonist of the first principle 'Eugenio', the second 'Constant', and their dialogue concerns the question of what *method* of learning can keep 'the Mind impenetrable to Prejudices and Mistakes, and to acquaint it with Philosophy and Science, without obliging it to go through the ordinary tedious Process, by which it is attained' (1757, p. 109).

The first answer is that of Eugenio:

> Instead of putting the Mind into a Mould, and hampering it with the Trammels of Education, in my opinion it would be better to give unlimited Scope to Nature, to lay no Bias on Judgement and Genius, to infuse no positive opinions;[10] but to let the young Adventurer, like the industrious bee, wander about in quest of intellectual Food, rifle every precious Flower and Blossom, and, after he has picked up Materials from every Quarter, range and digest them into a well-compacted and useful body. Such a Conduct would, I doubt not, produce more original Geniuses than we generally meet with; it would promote Invention, and enable the Mind, unbeaten and unsubdued by Art, to take amazing Flights into Regions hitherto unexplored.
> (*ibid.*, p. 110)

The second answer considers that this position will lead to some sort of 'non-education'. Education is not 'to set all things loose' which is only a 'fashionable Doctrine', not a concept (*ibid.*, p. 113).[11] Natural education is non-education, resulting in an untutored and uncultivated mind, whereas for education it is 'of the utmost Consequence to season young Minds with an early Tincture of Knowledge, as well as Virtue' (*ibid.*). 'Native Barbarity and Ignorance' can only be conquered if the 'unformed Creature' is 'taught the very first Principles of Human Knowledge, and the Arts of Civility' (*ibid.*, p. 114). The argument makes use of Locke's refutation of innate principles: 'We are told by Philosophers, of no small note, that the Mind is, at first, a kind of *Tabula Rasa*, or like a Piece of blank Paper, that bears no original Inscriptions, when we come into the World,—that we owe all the Characters afterwards drawn upon it, to the Impressions made upon our Senses; to Education, Custom, and the like.' Given this sensualistic principle it follows 'that a human Creature, untaught by Art, and undisciplined by Habit, does, of all other Creatures, lie the most open to Impressions from without, and is susceptible of every Form, Habit and Passion' (Fordyce, 1757, pp. 114, 115).

Locke had argued that 'custom settles habits of thinking in the understanding, as well as of determining the will, and the motions in the body' (Locke, 1976, p. 199). The 'Priestley principle' of learning favours the organization of habit formation and calls this the process of education. Fordyce presents the crucial argument for this:

even if a young mind is left as open as naturalists pleased with no culture applied, 'let Nature do all, will it form no opinions, contract no Habits?' (*ibid.*, p. 115). This must be denied, but then the idea of letting nature and the inner 'genius' grow becomes totally defective. What remains is an impressive alternative, 'either to leave him [the young mind] to himself, suck in such Notions, and contact such Habits, as his circumstances, and the uncertain Accidents of Life shall throw in his way; or to cultivate his Mind with Care, sow the Seeds of Knowledge and Virtue in it early, and improve his natural Talents by all the proper Arts of a liberal Education' (*ibid.*).

It was left to progressive education to show a way out of this standard argument, which was used as a legitimation for schooling and organized knowledge as opposed to genius and self-learning. Progressive education simply doubted the Lockean premiss of the whole argument for liberal education. The child's mind is not a *tabula rasa* but a living soul which develops its own faculties. Education is not another word for habit formation, that is a force of strong external influence, but must take into account the fact of *inner* development that all teaching can only follow and not alter.

CHILD-CENTRED EDUCATION

Shaftesbury favoured a 'balance' between the internal and the external: 'The inside Work is fitted to the outward Action and Performance' (1978, Vol. II, p. 135). The balance can be disturbed: 'Where Habits of Affections are dislodg'd, misplac'd or chang'd; where those belonging to one Species are intermixt with those belonging to another, there must of necessity be Confusion and Disturbance within' (*ibid.*, pp. 135,136). Given this, it follows that instruction is necessary, but only to form judgement and to exclude barbarity (1978, Vol. I, pp. 200, 222, 230). The soul cannot be formed but will form itself by developing its own style.

Progressive education seems to follow the same idea: education is helping the soul to develop, but no child can be 'formed' in the sensualistic manner, because the notion of development contradicts the assumption of a *tabula rasa*. 'Development' can only be thought of as an ordered (sequenced) movement out of *something*, not out of *nothing*. Locke's soul of the child was a *learned* soul (1976, p. 6), whereas progressive education in the nineteenth century started from Romantic sources, in particular from Froebel and the Froebel movement.[12] 'Soul' for Froebel was an intact and sacrosanct microcosm, a substantial divine inner life that develops itself constantly and through stages but from *one point* (Froebel, 1982, Vol. II, p. 24). The inner life must be structured because at the beginning it is 'an unarranged unmanifold entity' (*ibid.*, p. 34) but a living entity is not 'a piece of blank paper'. The child 'endeavours with his own active forces to constitute the inner life within a firm representation outside', that is, within *language* (*ibid.*), and this is no creation from outside but self-creation from within, a step-by-step development which is predetermined.

The concept of soul is central to most approaches of 'progressive education', Anglo-Saxon and continental. Even the label cannot deny its source: 'progression' originally meant development of the soul for which education can only lend support. The notion of 'soul' has a Christian heritage and this was revitalized by the Romantic movement of which Froebel was part. We can see a strong influence of Romantic concepts on education throughout the nineteenth century and the progressive movement emerged from this context. All its symbols, slogans and metaphors are of Romantic origin. The 'soul' of the child, education as 'gardening', the 'development' of 'germs'—the whole language of educational reform was impregnated with the Romantic idea of *growing*. Dewey's theory of 'reconstruction' did not really change this preoccupation.[13]

Romantic 'growth' has two clear advantages as a concept of education: it rules out indoctrination and opts for natural development, and therefore, so it seems, for the child's freedom. But 'growth' is a biological metaphor and implies necessity. Froebel spoke of a *divine law* that defines the necessary goodness of man, but not his freedom (1982, Vol. II, pp. 8 ff.). All development must refer to necessity and even determination, for otherwise there can be no sequential order and no forming of higher qualities. Freedom, on the other hand, must be linked to contingency, and this implies that it is a problematic educational concept. Freedom cannot just be the aim of education; at least this is what progressive education objected to in Kant, because his aim does not define the means of education. But if 'freedom' is more than just the formula for distant ends it will conflict with the Romantic notion of 'growth', and accordingly with the concept of 'soul' and the endogenous 'development' of all its faculties.

Freedom was the central concept of the most prominent 'progressive' educator of the twentieth century, Alexander Neill. His definition of 'freedom' resulted from a critique of authority. Freedom is what is left when we demolish authority in education: 'How . . . can I attempt to educate children when the ultimate solution of life is denied to me? I can only stand by and give them freedom to unfold. I do not know whither they are going, but that is all the more reason why I ought not to try to guide their footsteps. This is the final argument for the abolition of authority' (1920, p. 98).

But Neill also stresses determination, not by nature but by society. The child itself must be regarded as absolutely free, and is even allowed to act as an 'egoist', but society and especially the system of moral education represses his instincts (1929, p. 227, p. 45 and *passim*). 'This child brings with him a life force' that is a *natural* force which education does not allow to develop owing to 'a whole system of prohibitions' (1929, p. 15). The child is not good at heart but *selfish*, yet education cannot change this natural disposition.

> Altruism comes later, comes naturally if the child is not taught to be unselfish; probably never comes at all when the child is taught to be unselfish. . . . By suppressing the child's selfishness the mother is fixing that selfishness. An unfulfilled wish lives on in the unconsciousness. The child who is taught to be unselfish will remain selfish through life. Moral instruction thus defeats its own purpose.
> (*ibid.*, pp. 18, 19)

The strong influence of popular Freudianism can easily be spotted here, but this is not my point. Neill discusses the topic of *freedom* and *indoctrination* in a very suggestive, but nevertheless wrong way which is merely a variation of the Romantic syndrome. Freedom is derived from a *natural* force that no education can change except for the worse. All 'intentional' education is only repressive of nature; if nature is allowed to be expressed freely children will do no harm. They 'should be allowed almost infinite responsibility' but only under the supposition of a liberal environment (*ibid.*, p. 97).

When 'society accepts the notion that the child is all the better for being disciplined with fear' (Neill, 1939, p. 18), then schools can only be repressive and the repression will affect the whole nature of the child. But no school will repress *all* pupils and no repression is *total*, as Neill assumes. Only the idea that schools are 'closed' systems acting badly but effectively on pupils can make the argument solid because it suggests the need for a radical alternative, a non-repressive system, namely *Summerhill*.

Again an argument *pro domo*: 'Children come to me from disciplined schools, insincere little humbugs, with false manners which they drop in a week. Discipline and fear have made them act a part that is foreign to child nature, for a child is by nature a sincere little blighter' (*ibid.*, p. 42). But we respect the child, not his 'nature'. Neill's call for *respect* is a moral call using biological metaphors. What should be respected is the dignity of man, that is, of both children and grown-ups. Thus we respect the child as *man*, not as an undeveloped person and above all we cannot respect 'development' as such.

Neill treats biological metaphors literally and uses them as notions of obvious truth. This is what makes the appeal of progressive education so strong. Metaphors are treated as inner realities or deep structures of the soul. But Neill favours Freudian mechanics only negatively; they are used for *criticism* and not for a positive picture of the child. Here Neill is as Romantic as Froebel: education is growing and growing needs the right environment. Educators must be psychologists who have an insight into the souls of children. 'The teacher's chief concern should be the psychology of the child, and all school subjects should be relegated to an inferior place' (*ibid.*, p. 54).

Liberal education is seen as unhampered growing and studying is only a function of growth; it is no longer important in itself. But Neill's argument does not convince: he attacks school discipline and the indoctrination of the institution. But this *sociology* of education does not reveal any argument against liberal education. Neill and most progressive educators simply equate *knowledge* in education with *school* knowledge, artificial didactics, which may be useless but is itself only a special form of knowledge.[14] This form has been developed for the purposes of mass schooling and it can be changed only when the alternative will serve the same function. Neill offers an individualistic alternative and the question is whether it is tenable as a concept of schooling. But this again is not my point. The question of 'freedom' and 'indoctrination' is not reducible to a mere sociology of schooling. Also it is not a question of repressing the child's 'nature' or letting it grow. Rather it is what Neill *excluded* as a problem: in Summerhill all pupils have a free choice to learn whatever they are interested in, depending on what the school can offer. But should freedom of choice be allowed when this implies that crucial knowledge will be *missed*? The question that can be raised is what social organizations miss the least: the choice of a child or the adults' curriculum? We are thrown back to Fordyce's dialogue: is it sensible to 'set all things loose' in education or is responsibility to be accepted by organizing a curriculum of basic knowledge which is compulsory for everybody?

Neill is not interested in compulsory knowledge because he pictures a *natural* child that is led in the right direction by his own forces. In fact, Neill makes no distinction between natural intuition and the right choice. When the child makes an intuitive choice it will be a right one, because it is a *free*—that is, *uninfluenced*—choice. But 'force', the key notion of the eighteenth-century psychology of education, very influential for Pestalozzi and others, is a *physical* concept that does not describe either psychological laws or educational processes.[15] Neill overlooked the physical basis of Freudian theory partly because of his friendship with Wilhelm Reich, who strongly follows the idea of inner 'forces' and 'drives' that can be described in terms of psycho-physiology (see Sulloway, 1979).[16] But the development of a child cannot be reduced to physiological factors. On the other hand neither is it just an organic process, unconnected with the acquisition of knowledge. Rather 'development' is the *autopoiesis* of understanding, a mental 'growing in' that includes biological processes but cannot be reduced to them.[17]

This process is not possible without knowledge, and Fordyce was right: we only have the choice to organize and influence the process or relinquish it to somebody else. The school organization can be more or less 'liberal' but this cannot mean that children are free *not* to learn. One can refuse knowledge but not deny it, because one cannot deny understanding. In this liberal education is right and the child-centred opponents are wrong, or rather they have missed the point.

FREEDOM AND INDOCTRINATION

Schools are social organizations and as such they cannot be 'free' in an absolute sense. Summerhill had its rules, even authorities, and was different only as a new and alternative form of organization. I will not argue against that form because school reform is an open process and it may well be that future schools will have much more in common with Neill's 'Summerhill' (or the anti-establishment institutions of progressive education) than Neill himself ever expected (see Oelkers, 1989). But what is crucial to every reform is the definition of its *purpose*. And here we seem to have an alternative which can lead only into a vicious circle. Education needs organization but organization contradicts the nature of the child. Genius, inner form or soul must develop independently but needs knowledge, which in turn, however, needs organization, and so on.

Neill said of 'reform' teachers that their basic attitude is wrong: 'Their interest was in education, not in children. They had a scheme of life, and they tried to make the child fit to it . . . . They were wrong because they depended on educating the conscious mind of a child' (1929, p. 211).[18] But it is exactly this that education should do, not by fixing the mind to a scheme but by initiating the mind into the world of knowledge.[19] The process of education can be realized in different ways but cannot be avoided. One cannot choose to be educated or not, but what education will do cannot be defined strictly.[20] The notion 'education' does not refer to a natural force or a social instrument and therefore the process cannot be a process of determination that is not alterable. Nature (even development) may be determined, but not education if it is understood in terms of action theory. 'Educating' means *acting*, and human acts are not derived from natural laws but have to do with intentions and are therefore uncertain. The acting may be specified, but the outcome is not, because it is not 'produced' by education. 'To give a child ideals is a dangerous thing to do. No man is good enough to give another his own ideals' (*ibid.*). But this holds only if we suppose that giving ideals once will *fix* the child's mind and habit *for ever*. Progressive education warns against the danger of indoctrination, referring only to the *act* not to the *process* of education or to the process as a *negative* determination. But education must be designed as a process with an uncertain outcome. Giving ideals often cannot be avoided but the act as such does not imply direct and long-term effective indoctrination. Neill and other progressives suggest that one act or one situation will have consequences that cannot be altered unless progressive education is implemented. But even repressive schools can never have effects that are totally unique. All effects of education spread and all effects can lead to paradoxes (see Oelkers, 1982). Giving ideals can be as dangerous as *not* giving ideals; but even worse, giving ideals in one case can have no effect, in other cases can have effects other than those intended, and so on.

Strike formulates the problem as a paradox: 'People are born free: as moral agents they have the duty to be the authors of their own thoughts. Yet people who would be competent thinkers must commit themselves to mastery of the tools, and this requires submission to a conceptual heritage' (1982, p. 70). This is, of course, a restatement of the Priestley principle and it still cannot avoid attacks from the Shaftesbury principle movement. One can always regard learning that requires 'submission to a conceptual heritage' as 'indoctrination' if the inner self is regarded as free and sacrosanct in a way that does not necessarily require knowledge. But then all learning must be regarded as 'indoctrination' because learning requires the acquiring of knowledge. And the point for progressive education is whether everyday life demands a stronger or weaker repression than schooling. But the problem is still more complicated: if there is a desire and a decision to learn something above the level of everyday understanding, *submission* is *necessary* because the learner cannot judge what he is learning before the end of the process. Learning will change the whole conception of knowledge and the learner can only *intend* this to be a change for the better. In this he is *not free*. His decision to learn can be free but after that he must bind himself to a corpus of knowledge as a condition for teaching and learning. Thus learning requires authority, not necessarily that of teachers but that of traditions. The learner can alter traditions but only *after* he becomes initiated into them. He can also ignore traditions but then he must consider himself as not competent. This might be called the freedom of ignorance but it would be freedom on hypothetical grounds. *Knowing* of ignorance is a paradox but at the same time shows the necessity of education. There is no state of innocence called 'ignorance' because one cannot avoid knowledge. Ignorance may be a state of poor knowledge mixed with uninterest, but there is no freedom in it, only the possibility of stopping a certain kind of learning.

Indoctrination in education can be accepted in the case of political and economic influences or deprivations that result from social structures which are often not intended but nevertheless effective. *Beyond Domination* (White, 1983) can be read as a process of democratization and participation even in schools (1983, p. 92). But still we have not solved the problem whether learning itself can be regarded as indoctrination because all learning must refer to authoritative traditions of knowledge. This is the case not only in relation to forms of schooling, but to every socialization of mind, because the forming of understanding will take place regardless of whether there are special didactical arrangements or not. Everyday life is an ongoing growth of understanding and therefore socialization of mind, and the only question is whether this offers the *best* chance for the child.

Interest is not a natural 'force'. The motivation for learning can have many sources but all of them are part of socialization. 'Socialization' means for the child that he is confronted with knowledge from the beginning of his tentative understanding. The application of knowledge leads to understanding but at the same time to *not* understanding. Thus children ask questions to solve the puzzles of *not* understanding.

And this is the crucial point of the whole process: 'The virtues involved in not knowing are the ones that really count in the long run. What you do about what you don't know is, in the final analysis, what determines what you will ultimately know' (Duckworth, 1987, p. 68). Parents and teachers can help children to develop the virtues of knowing when they respect the process of learning out of *not* knowing (*ibid.*, p. 69). But must this process be compulsory? The question of whether the state has a right to enforce a minimum of education for everybody must be separated from the question of whether education must be regarded as indoctrination. The first question allows pragmatic solutions, the second does not. If we regard the right to education as one of the fundamental human rights then education must be offered to everybody. This offer must be organized and paid for and when there are better alternatives than those under state control, these alternatives should be realized. But all this political discussion makes sense only when we regard education itself as legitimate. Education *as* indoctrination would be *not* legitimate, but liberal education pretends to *form* the mind and it looks as if this must be called 'indoctrination' too. The mind cannot resist the forming when the process of education takes place, and it must take place because human learning is related to human culture. At least in some aspects culture represents authority for the learner; at the beginning of education the learner has no choice, he cannot decide *against* education which, on the other hand, strongly influences him. So how can we defend this and not call it 'indoctrination'? If we abandon all connotations of 'natural education', that is, the development of germs in what Froebel called the garden of education, then we have only *one* criterion for whether education is indoctrination or not, the criterion of *understanding* (see Oelkers, 1985).

Education is indoctrination when it has the power to fix habits or dispositions without the participation of the child's active powers. But the mind is not a sensualistic *tabula rasa*, rather a self-constructive hemisphere that is built up by structuring experience through knowledge, that is, understanding. Liberal education is *not* indoctrination if it is helpful in this process. 'Helpful', however, has two sides, an empirical and a more transcendental: the building up of understanding is necessary and unavoidable, but so is helping. One can ignore a child's question but if the question is to be answered it can only be done in a *helpful* way. At least we have no possibility of justifying other ways of answering. Empirically there are different ways because what helps can be different. One can answer in a 'child-oriented' way but this can be the wrong strategy because it leaves no room for further questions; on the other hand an 'adult' answer can be unhelpful because the child does not understand it. But the misunderstood answer can be what is really challenging, and so on.

If we adopt categories of inner 'genius' or 'natural' development then all education can be considered as indoctrination. But we cannot avoid talking with the child, giving ideals or reasoning. Thus we cannot avoid presenting knowledge. Whatever the inner state of children may be it is always 'impregnated' with knowledge, otherwise no understanding would be possible. Education may 'disturb' the inner self (Luhmann, 1987) but two things can be excluded: education is not an *instrument* to produce mental states or inner dispositions and education is not a *linear* process to reach distant aims. The equation of education with indoctrination stems from these two suppositions; when they become indefensible the equation has to be abandoned.

But the process can still be called 'indoctrination' if we have in mind the picture of the natural genius that knows best what is best for knowing. But the Priestley principle has at least sound objections: knowing is the effect of learning, not the opposite, and knowledge can be altered by further learning; indoctrinated beliefs can be corrected, at least in most cases. Indoctrination would be much stronger if liberal education were to be excluded because the child's mind is not a map of reasoning but a map-in-being.[21] And this has to do with both the open and the secret ways of understanding.

So I can conclude: there is no *contradiction* between 'freedom' and 'education' because education will not necessarily lead to *indoctrination*. On the other hand, nor can education produce 'freedom'. Liberal education can try to promote the development of the mind, but basically it is a process of self-promotion that can or must be helped by education.

Thus at the same time Kant's paradox can be solved *and* confirmed: it is legitimate to cultivate freedom and at the same time put constraints on the child if we have in mind processes of liberal education which demand liberal forms of teaching. Knowledge forms the mind, but only in a free way; at the same time all forming of mind is a kind of bondage to cultural heritage. The result might be *new* knowledge, but all knowledge can only be educationally transmitted as a restriction of (personal) freedom. This restriction, fashioned as an organized but fair process of learning (not as an act of the teacher's arbitrariness), cannot be called coercion if it serves the freedom of judgement. If not, education is illegitimate.

NOTES

(1)   'Wie kultiviere ich die Freiheit bei dem Zwang' (Kant, 1964, p. 711). The best reading of this paradox is Vogel (1990).

(2)   'On Genius' was first published in the *Monthly Repository* in October 1832 under the pseudonym 'Antiquus'.

(3)   Thomas Elyot wrote that it is 'Knowledge which maketh a Wise Man' (quoted in Bantock, 1980, p. 98).

(4)   This is discussed in Mill's *Logic* (1973/1974 Book III, Ch. 5, part 4).

(5)   'All men are liable to mistake in deciding on genius at a very early age; but parents more than all, from their natural partiality' (Knox, 1784, p. 224).

(6)   Moral sense cannot be taught because of its aesthetic quality' (Shaftesbury, 1978, Vol. II, p. 41 ff.).

(7)   Enlightenment is virtually unlimited, as a French observer wrote in 1786: 'Il ne manque aux enfans que deux chose pour bien raisoner; l'attention, & l'expérience' (Flevry, 1786, p. 95).

(8)   Recommended subjects of teaching are civil history and civil policy, 'such as the theory of laws, government, manufactures, commerce, naval force, etc.' (Priestley, 1778, p. 196).

(9)   Priestley published his 'Essay on a Course of Liberal Education for Civil and Active Life' in 1760 (reprinted in Priestley, 1778, pp. 185–229). The third edition of Fordyce's *Dialogues Concerning Education* appeared in 1757. Nevertheless Fordyce discussed two well-known principles, of which the second was fully formulated some years later by Priestley.

(10)   Written or published five years *before* Rousseau's *Education négative* (1762).

(11)   The doctrine goes: 'Let us once get free of all Principles and Restraints, and then our Practice may take its full swing' (Fordyce, 1757, p. 113).

(12)   Froebel's theory is discussed in Bantock (1984, Ch. 4); see also Selleck (1968). The

American 'Kindergarten' movement is mentioned in Cremin (1980, pp. 388 ff.).

(13)   Dewey's influence on progressive education has been strong in academic theory but significantly weaker in practical orientation; here we find the language and the concepts of the nineteenth century. I am indebted to M. Knoll for his comments on this subject.

(14)   But this is an empirical question: even repressive schooling can be of use, at least negatively; but what repressive schooling 'is', cannot, as Neill does, be taken as self-evident.

(15)   This was of course the idea of Wundt, who differentiated between physical and psychological causality, but this was regarded by Neill (1929, pp. 210, 211) as not being part of 'modern', that is Freudian, psychology.

(16)   The friendship is documented in Placzek (1981); for details see Croall (1983).

(17)   I owe the idea of 'growing in' to M. Langeveld (1968).

(18)   German educators whom he met during his stay at Hellerau, a reform school near Dresden. Neill stayed there for more than two years (1921–3). (For information on Hellerau I am indebted to J. Helmchen.)

(19)   The concept 'education as initiation' is usually attributed to R. S. Peters, but the term was used in German education earlier (see Flitner, 1961, p. 42); the idea derives from neo-humanism and was theorized by German *geisteswissenschaftliche Pädagogik* after the First World War (see Oelkers, 1990).

(20)   One can call this a *pragmatic a priori*: education must happen, because one cannot avoid acting with children and these actions cannot but be qualified morally. In short: one cannot act for the *worse* of the child, only for the best.

(21)   Ryle's famous metaphor—mind as a map or the 'logical geography of concepts'—misses one point; one geography can be exchanged for another, a mind must 'develop'.

REFERENCES

Bacon, F. (1975) *The Advancement of Learning* (1605), Book I, ed. W. A. Armstrong. London: The Athlone Press.

Bantock, G. H. (1980, 1984) *Studies in History of Educational Theory*. Vol. I: *Artifice and Nature, 1350–1765*; Vol. II: *The Minds and the Masses, 1760–1980*. London, Boston and Sydney: Allen & Unwin.

Chapone, Mrs (1783) *Letters on the Improvement of the Mind Addressed to a Young Lady*, a new edition. London: J. Walter/C. Dilly.

Cremin, L. A. (1980) *American Education: The National Experience 1783–1876*. New York: Harper & Row.

Croall, J. (1983) *Neill of Summerhill: The Permanent Rebel*. London, Melbourne/Henley: Routledge & Kegan Paul.

Duckworth, E. (1987) The having of wonderful ideas. In *Other Essays on Teaching and Learning*. New York and London: Teachers College, Columbia University.

Elyot, T. (1962) *The Book Named The Governor* (1531), ed. S. E. Lehmberg. London: Everyman's Library.

Flevry, C. (1786) *Traité du choix et de la méthode des études*. Paris: Piere Aubin *et al.*

Flitner, W. (1961) *Die gymnasiale Oberstufe*. Heidelberg: Quelle & Meyer.

Fordyce, D. (1757) *Dialogues Concerning Education*, Vol. I, 3rd edn. London: E. Dilly.

Froebel, F. (1982) *Augewählte Schriften*, Vol. II: *Die Menschenerziehung*, ed. E. Hoffmann, 4th ed. Stuttgart: Klett-Cotta.

Kant, I. (1964) Ueber Pädagogik. In *I. Kant: Werke*, ed. W. Weischedel, Vol. XII, pp. 691–761. Frankfurt: Insel-Verlag.

Knox, V. (1784) *Liberal Education or, A Practical Treatise on the Methods of Acquiring Useful and Polite Learning*, 6th edn. London: C. Dilly.

Langeveld, M. J. (1968) *Studien zur Anthropologie des Kindes*, 3rd rev. and augm. edn (Forschungen zür Pädagogik und Anthropologie, ed. O. F. Bollnow, W. Flitner and A. Nitschke, Vol. 1. Tübingen: V. Niemeyer.

Locke, J. (1976) *An Essay Concerning Human Understanding* (1690), abr. and ed. J. W. Yolton. London and Melbourne: Everyman's Library.
Luhmann, N. (1987) Strukturelle Defizite. Bemerkungen zur systemtheoretischen Analyse des Erziehungswesens. In J. Oelkers and H. E. Tenorth (eds) *Pädagogik, Erziehungswissenschaft und Systemtheorie*, pp. 57–75. Basle: Weinheim.
Mill, J. S. (1965) On genius (1832). In J. S. Mill, *Essays on Literature and Society*, ed. J.B. Scheewind, pp. 87–101. New York and London: Collier-Macmillan.
Mill, J. S. (1973, 1974) *A System of Logic Ratiocinative and Inductive. Being a Connected View of the Principles of Evidence and the Methods of Scientific Investigations* Books I–II, IV–VI and Appendices, 2 vols, ed. J. M. Robson. Introduction by R. F. McRae. Toronto, Buffalo and London: University of Toronto Press, Routledge & Kegan Paul.
Mill, J. S. (1974) *On Liberty* (1859), ed. G. Himmelfarb. Harmondsworth, Middlesex: Penguin Books.
Neill, A. S. (1920) *A Dominie in Doubt*. London: Herbert Jenkins.
Neill, A. S. (1929) *The Problem Child*, new edn with appendix. London: Herbert Jenkins.
Neill, A. S. (1939) *The Problem Teacher*. London: Herbert Jenkins.
Oelkers, J. (1985) Intention und Wirkung. Vorüberlegungen zu einer Theorie pädagogischen Handelns. In N. Luhmann and K.E. Schorr (eds) *Zwischen Technologie und Selbstreferenz. Fragen an die Pädagogik*, pp. 139–194. Frankfurt: Suhrkamp.
Oelkers, J. (1986) Verstehen als Bildungsziel. In N. Luhmann and K.E. Schorr (eds) *Zwischen Intransparenz und Verstehen. Fragen an die Pädagogik*, pp. 167–218. Frankfurt: Suhrkamp.
Oelkers, J. (1989) *Reformpädagogik—Eine kritische Dogmengeschichte*. Munich and Weinheim: Juventa.
Oelkers, J. (1991) *Hermeneutik oder Kulturpädagogik: Zur Bilanzierung der geisteswissen-schaftlichen Pädagogik*. Weinheim: Deutscher Studien Verlag.
Placzek, B. R. (ed.) (1981) *Record of a Friendship. The Correspondence of Wilhelm Reich and A. S. Neill*. New York: Farrar, Straus & Giroux.
Priestley, J. (1778) *Miscellaneous Observations Relating to Education. Most Especially, as it Respects the Conduct of the Mind. To Which is Added, An Essay on a Course of Liberal Education for Civil and Active life*. Bath: R. Cruttwell.
Selleck, R. J. W. (1968) *The New Education, 1870–1914*. London: Pitman.
Shaftesbury, A. A. C. (1978) *Characteristicks of Men, Manners, Opinions, Times*, in Three Volumes (London, 1711). Hildesheim and New York: Georg Olms.
Sheridan, T. (1769) *British Education: Or, The Source of the Disorders of Great Britain. Being An Essay Towards Proving, that the Immorality, Ignorance, and False Taste, which so Generally Prevail, Are the Natural and Necessary Consequences of the Present Defective System of Education. A New Edition, revised by the Author, with Additions and Alterations*. London: E. and C. Dilly.
Strike, K. A. (1982) *Liberty and Learning*. Oxford: Martin Robertson.
Sulloway, F. J. (1979) *Freud, Biologist of the Mind: Beyond the Psychoanalytic Legend*. New York: Basic Books.
Vogel, P. (1990) *Kausalität und Freiheit in der Pädagogik Studien im Anschluss an die Freiheitsantinomie bei Kant*. Frankfurt, Berne, New York and Paris: Lang.
Warnock, M. (1988) *A Common Policy for Education*. Oxford and New York: Oxford University Press.
White, J. P. (1973) *Towards a Compulsory Curriculum*. London, Henley and Boston: Routledge & Kegan Paul.
White, P. (1983) *Beyond Domination, An Essay in the Political Philosophy of Education*. London, Boston, Melbourne and Henley: Routledge & Kegan Paul.
Williams, D. (1774) *A Treatise on Education. In Which the General Method Pursued in the Public Institutions of Europe; and Particularly in those of England; that of Milton, Locke, Rousseau and Helvetius are considered; and a more practicable and useful one proposed*. London: T. Payne, E. & C. Dilly et al.

Chapter 8

The Justification of Autonomy as an Educational Aim

John White

Personal autonomy, in the shape of self-directedness in the conduct of one's life, is a central value in a liberal democratic society. Its promotion has been urged by many writers as an important aim of education in such a society.

How can this aim be justified? In this chapter I shall look first at a discussion of this question in Eamonn Callan's recent book *Autonomy and Schooling* (1988). The second section will examine Joseph Raz's account of the value of personal autonomy (in general, not specifically as an educational aim) in his *Morality of Freedom* (1986). In the final section I will take up the issue of the education of children in minority communities which do not value the autonomous life.

CALLAN'S ARGUMENT

Callan looks at a number of arguments for the value of autonomy.

(1) He examines first an *instrumental* justification, that autonomy is desirable because it leads to happiness. His objection is that it does not always do so. In a society with extensive freedom, where people have the opportunity of creating the meaning of their lives, 'their happiness is likely to be fragile at best if they have little realism or independence of mind' (1988, p. 41). But we can still ask if this kind of society is desirable. In tradition-directed communities people can lead contented lives with very little room for individual discretion. 'The development of tradition-directed communities which fit that description does not seem to be an unfeasible aspiration' (*ibid.*).

Callan seems to be assuming here that a valid justification must apply *universally*, that is, across both tradition-directed and non-tradition-directed societies. Otherwise he could not appeal to the experience of people living in a tradition-directed society as a counter-example. But is this so? Need the justification of autonomy show that it is valuable for *every human being*? He also claims it is a feasible aspiration to develop tradition-directed communities. Is it? We shall be returning to both these points later.

(2) He then turns to an argument *from the absence of ethical experts*. The argument runs like this. There are no experts on what the good life should consist in. No one is in a proper position to lay down to other individuals how they should lead their lives. So people should be left to lead their own lives, that is, autonomously. Callan's objection to this is that if one accepts the premiss that there are no experts on the good life, it does not follow that autonomy is a good thing: 'we have no reason to believe that pupils who become highly autonomous will be better placed to make the right decision than those who unthinkingly follow orders' (p. 41). So there is still something arbitrary about acting autonomously.

Callan is assuming that there *is* a right decision to be made. Is there? Is it indeed appropriate to talk of a 'right decision' here? What does it mean? Further, Callan has already conceded that in a non-tradition-directed society like our own, autonomy may well promote happiness. So it may not be arbitrary in our context to urge autonomy, if, that is, the promotion of happiness is an acceptable reason.

(3) Callan's positive argument begins from the claim that autonomy is intrinsically valuable, but that not all intrinsically valuable things in life are experiences. He refers to Nozick's example of a machine that stimulates in the brain whatever experiences we desire, for example the experience of scientific discovery, winning a match or making love, claiming that we would regard these experiences as a poor substitute for the real thing. As he says, this shows that experiences are intrinsically valuable, but it does not show that autonomy is. At this point he refers to Nozick's further idea of a transformation machine which can turn us into whatever kind of person we wish to become; and a results machine that changes the world in any direction we wish. We still would not want to live our lives plugged into these machines, because they would be leading our lives for us: we would not be living our own lives. 'We live our own lives to the extent that the experiences we have, the kind of persons we become, and the changes we make to the world flow from the exercise of personal autonomy' (p. 44).

How far does this justify personal autonomy? Suppose we agree that everyone would prefer a life that they led themselves to a life plugged into Nozick's machines: this does not imply that all who so choose will be personally autonomous. Callan contrasts the autonomous person with the tradition-directed person. But a tradition-directed person may well also reject the machines. He may want his life to flow from his own choices. True, what he chooses to do will be in accordance with tradition, but even so, his life is governed by his choices, not by a machine.

Following Gray (1983, p. 74), we need to distinguish what has been called the *autarchic* person from the *autonomous* person. An autarchic person enjoys negative freedom from force and coercion, and is also rationally self-determining, in that he has engaged in rational deliberation on the alternatives open to him. One can be autarchic, at least to some extent, in a tradition-directed society. Traditions do not always minutely specify what one should do: there is room for rational deliberation and choice. An autonomous person has the features of the autarchic person, but 'must also have distanced himself in some measure from the conventions of his social environment and from the influence of the people surrounding him. His actions express principles and policies which he has himself ratified by a process of critical reflection' (Gray, 1983, p. 74).

Callan may have given us grounds why autarchy is valuable—that is, that no one would want to live without it since the desire for it is deeply embedded in everyone's desire structure. But this says nothing about why autonomy is desirable. Why is it a good thing to distance oneself from conventions, to live a critically reflective life?

(One finds a similar conflation of autonomy and autarchy in Richard Lindley, who writes: 'A is conatively heteronomous with respect to a particular action or set of actions if either A acts through domination by lower order desires, or A acts through weakness of will' (1986, p. 70). On this view a sufficient condition of acting autonomously is that one lives by the desires one desires to rule one, not by lower-order desires or desires one would rather be without. But, once again, this would make a well-brought-up, virtuous member of a tradition-directed community an autonomous person—even though he never questioned the conventions in which he had been brought up.)

The basic problem in Callan's positive argument is echoed in the account of the pupil's good that I spelt out in White (1982, Ch. 3). I claimed there that personal autonomy is a necessary feature of human flourishing and that its promotion is required in any education which seeks to cultivate the pupil's well-being. But my argument for this was weak. Just as Callan begins from Nozick's experience machine, I focused on Huxley's *Brave New World*. If we reject the picture of human flourishing given in that book, why do we do so?

> But what, after all, is wrong with Brave New World, if anything is? Many would say it is that its inhabitants have not been given the autonomy to determine their own lives for themselves: they have been *conditioned* to lead a life of constant pleasure and have not chosen this themselves.
> (1982, p. 39)

But the rejection of 'Brave New World' does not necessarily spring from considerations of autonomy. For the autarchic member of a tradition-directed society would also oppose it—just as he would spurn the experience machine.

To return to Callan. We may conclude that his positive justification for autonomy does not work, except by weakening the notion of autonomy so that it is no more than autarchy. In addition, the justifications he rejects have not been conclusively shown to be inadequate. Taken together, his arguments raise the question: how far should we be looking for a justification of autonomy of a universal type, that is, one which shows it to be a good for every human being? If we take this line can we get farther than justifying autarchy rather than autonomy?

RAZ'S ARGUMENT

We need a new starting point. Joseph Raz (1986, pp. 390–5) discusses the value of personal autonomy. Earlier in the book he argues, convincingly in my view, that personal autonomy is not a necessary feature of personal well-being in general. He defines personal well-being partly in terms of a life (or part of a life) in which one's major goals have been realized, that is, those desires which are most important to one in the hierarchy of one's desires. So a person in a tradition-directed society could lead a life of great well-being. Suppose he wants above all to be a good carpenter, a good father, to be highly regarded in the community, generous, temperate, etc.

If all this comes to pass, he may on this view be said to achieve a high measure of personal well-being.

Raz sees personal autonomy as having to do with a particular ideal of the good life. He writes

> In western industrial societies a particular conception of individual well-being has acquired considerable popularity. It is the ideal of personal autonomy. It transcends the conceptual point that personal well-being is partly determined by success in willingly endorsed pursuits and holds the free choice of goals and relations as an essential ingredient of individual well-being. The ruling idea of personal autonomy is that people should make their own lives. The autonomous person is a (part) author of his own life. The ideal of personal autonomy is the vision of people controlling, to some degree, their own destiny, fashioning it through successive decisions throughout their lives.
> (1986, p. 369)

He goes on to say that

> It is an ideal particularly suited to the conditions of the industrial age and its aftermath with their fast changing technologies and free movement of labour. They call for an ability to cope with changing technological, economic and social conditions, for an ability to adjust, to acquire new skills, to move from one sub-culture to another, to come to terms with new scientific and moral views.
> (pp. 369–70)

Although there have been autonomous people in past ages, autonomy is an ideal of life particularly favoured in our own culture.

Attending to the kind of justification of the ideal that Raz provides, we see that, unlike Callan, he does not try to show that it is good universally, that is, for any human being: in a tradition-directed society it is *not* a component of individual well-being. Raz wants to argue that for *us*, in a non-tradition-directed society, autonomy helps us to flourish.

How does Raz deal with the objection that this is only true of those of us who make autonomy one of our major goals in life? How can it be good for those who do not include it among their major goals? He replies that this assumes that autonomy is one goal among others: writing poetry, bringing up a family, making a fortune. . .being autonomous. But it is not like this. Being autonomous is not one goal among others. It is tied more closely to features of the kind of society in which we live. His general conclusion is that

> For those of us who live in an autonomy-supporting environment there is no choice but to be autonomous: there is no other way to prosper in such a society.
> (p. 391)

This introduces the notion of an 'autonomy-supporting environment'. I need to say a few words about what Raz takes this to be. His point is that the social institutions among which we live are constituted on the assumption that people will be leading a broadly autonomous life (given that the latter can be a matter of degree). They may have their counterparts in tradition-directed societies, but the latter are not built on the assumption mentioned. Take marriage as an example. In our society marriage is built on the assumption that people will independently choose whom they will marry, rather than on the assumption of prearrangement. Similar points can be made about choice of occupation or place of residence. Generally, we are brought up in a culture whose major institutions are premised on the ideal of personal autonomy. Within this framework there may be variations in the extent to which people welcome making choices. Some may 'base more of their lives on those aspects, such as parenthood, where choice is more limited' (p. 394). So some people may lead less autonomous lives than others. But broadly speaking, 'ultimately those who live in an autonomy-enhancing culture can prosper only by being autonomous' (*ibid.*)

Raz's account of the value of autonomy is attractive, but I have one reservation. Recall Gray's description of autonomy, quoted earlier: 'an autonomous agent must also have distanced himself in some measure from the conventions of his social environment and from the influence of the people surrounding him' (1983, p. 74). Now it is true that people in our kind of society are not directed by convention or authority in the selection of marriage partners, occupation or place of residence. (We might add to these the selection of types of food or domestic goods, non-work activities, and no doubt other things.) But the institutions to do with marriage, work, residence, consumer choice and so on within which we flourish themselves embody conventions. It would be quite easy for people in our kind of society to make choices within these areas, yet never to reflect on the conventional structure itself.

I heard the other day of a young woman who works as a home help in the day and as a security officer in a company at night, snatching a little sleep in the afternoons. She is saving up for her wedding in December. Her dress will cost her £1000 and she is inviting 700 guests. At the same time she has cut herself off from all interest in the outside world beyond her immediate family and friends. She has no idea what is going on in the wider world and does not care. As she says, she lives only for herself and sees nothing wrong with this.

Although the details of her case may be unusual, there are many people in our society, I suggest, who have broadly the same attitude to life. They delight in the fact that they can make their own choices about how they are going to live—about their marriage arrangements, jobs, even patterns of sleeping and waking. But are such people autonomous if they simply *accept* the conventional structures around them and never question them? It is possible to imagine a version of Huxley's 'Brave New World', in which people are not genetically programmed and conditioned as in that book, but are encouraged to live a life of abundant choice-making, yet are still manipulated by an elite to be docile and unquestioning.

We seem to be dealing with a weaker and a stronger sense of 'personal autonomy'. The difference between them is that the stronger sense, but not the weaker, requires critical reflectiveness about basic social structures. If this is so, then Raz's argument for the value of autonomy certainly seems to work for the weaker sense, in that in order to flourish we must (broadly) make various choices in our lives as encouraged by the choice-supporting institutions among which we live. But does his argument support personal autonomy in the stronger sense? Has he shown that it helps us to flourish to be critically reflective about our basic social institutions? This is where I am more doubtful.

In Raz's defence one might point to institutions other than the ones he has concentrated on, like marriage and work—to political institutions and perhaps to the education system, which might be said to be autonomy-supporting in the stronger sense of the term.

Take the political system. We live in a liberal democracy. This implies that citizens do not simply accept whatever government happens to rule over them, but choose what they consider to be the best government in the light of critical reflection on alternatives. Similarly, it may be argued that part of our understanding of what our educational system is about is that it helps to produce critically reflective people. For some thinkers, John Anderson for instance, this aim is written definitionally into the meaning of 'education'.

How powerful is this possible defence of Raz? One might reply that it is not impressive as an account of what our political and educational institutions are actually like—as distinct from some idealized picture of what they might be.

When people vote, is this in the light of critical reflection on the kinds of social institutions they want? On a Schumpeterian account of democracy, there is certainly choice involved—autonomy in the weaker sense. But the choice is between competing elites, all of which are committed to the maintenance of the social structure as it is. So there is no support here, on this view, for autonomy in the stronger sense. As for the educational system—as it is, not in an idealized sense—there is no need to outline the evidence that while pupils are certainly encouraged, at least in many instances, to work hard at their science, maths, languages and so on in order to promote their life chances—and hence their autonomy in the weaker sense—there is not generally the same pressure to encourage them to be critically reflective about their society as a whole. Political education does not have the same status within the system, to put it ludicrously mildly, as science or mathematics.

Can we conclude, then, that we do *not* live in an autonomy-supporting society in the stronger sense? Not so quickly. We cannot assume that the character of our political and educational institutions is manifested only in what happens within them in practice. On the political side, it is often said that we live in an imperfect democracy. Perhaps many voters *do* choose between party elites according to which can best produce economic goods. But this is not all that those who over the centuries have forged our democratic system have had in mind. They have had something more like the stronger autonomy ideal in mind—a vision of self-determining citizens, aware of ideological obfuscations which can make them *seem* independent agents, even though they are victims of subtle manipulation.

Similarly in education. It is part of the liberal democratic ideal in general that young people are brought up equipped and disposed to play their part in a democratic society. This would involve their acquiring a good deal of knowledge of their society and other society, as well as various virtues, like independence of thought, political courage or concern for others in the community. On this view a school system which paid no attention to this, or made it harder for pupils to acquire these achievements, would be a perversion of the democratic ideal.

Also according this view one must attend to, as it were, the inner logic of our political and educational institutions, not just their outward forms. They go with a picture of a society in which these logical requirements are more fully realized. This would be a society in which citizens voted in full understanding of the issues at stake, were roughly equal in political power, exercised their democratic dispositions not only in national and local government but in all aspects of their lives, including their workplaces. It would be a society in which part of everyone's education would prepare them for life in liberal democratic institutions of these sorts.

If it is allowed that our political and educational institutions carry with them such a social vision, it makes much more sense to see them as autonomy-supporting in the stronger sense.

If it is allowed. . . .The question remains how far it is legitimate to extrapolate in this way from the actual to the ideal. Certainly, if we come back to the central issue of whether individuals need the stronger kind of autonomy in order to flourish, we have to take them as we find them, shaped by the avowedly imperfect political and educational institutions among which they have grown up. It is still not at all clear why they cannot flourish if they lack reflectiveness about their society. If flourishing has to do with fulfilling one's major goals in life, then why must such fulfilment bring with it this reflectiveness?

Let us try one more way—not, at least initially, based on Raz's argument about an autonomy-supporting society—of showing that personal autonomy in the stronger sense is a condition of flourishing. Strong autonomy can make one alert to possible ways in which one's flourishing may be frustrated—by manipulation, for instance, or political tyranny. But is being autonomous helpful to *everyone* in this way? Much may depend on how one construes personal flourishing or well-being.

Suppose this is conceived in a highly individualistic way, such that, in order to flourish, the individual need not be concerned with promoting others' well-being. A person may, for instance, be interested in pursuing a musical career and be quite prepared to work within the social framework in which she finds herself: she simply does not want to think about this. Is it necessarily in her interests to become reflective about social institutions? She is certainly concerned about removing obstacles to her well-being, but these are things like not having enough to live on, falling ill, having too little time to practise. Need she go further than this?

Suppose, on the other hand, we are working with a conception of personal well-being that embraces concern for others, at both intimate and less intimate levels: it is now part of my own flourishing that I promote the flourishing of my friends and of others—strangers—within the groups and communities within which I find myself. Here I do not know what might be obstacles to these people's flourishing. I have a far less determinate picture of this than the musician had in the earlier example. Among the new obstacles may be political ones, like manipulation, authoritarianism, the power of sectional interests: the broader concern for others' well-being leads one thus to have a broader view of possible obstacles.

It would take another paper to discuss whether personal well-being is better conceived in the altruistic way. (My own view, to put it telegrammatically, is that while there is no logical necessity about this, there are good reasons why educators—parents and teachers—should bring children up within this more generous conception of their well-being.) As far as the value of autonomy in the stronger sense goes, the conclusion is that this is more clearly visible if one works with the wider rather than the narrower conception of well-being. It *may* be true that one is also better off in the more individualistic sense if one is autonomous; but this is less clearly apparent.

But let us press this last point further. Could the musician in our example flourish, after all, without social reflectiveness? Flourishing is a matter of degree. Would she flourish more with reflectiveness? How far is it true that she can identify obstacles to her well-being without it? The difficulty is that whatever category of obstacle we think of, it is hard to seal this off from wider social and political concerns. Understanding what might promote or harm one's health, for instance, cannot but lead one, in our kind of society, into considerations of public health policy, pollution, advertising and food-processing methods. Similar points could be made about other vital needs—for shelter, clothing, security against personal injury, theft or deceit, freedom of thought and action, social recognition, and others. There is no consensus in our kind of open society about how such conditions of flourishing can best be guaranteed. Given that it is in anyone's interests to think about such matters, it is impossible to avoid the controversies that abound in all these areas. Reflectiveness is, after all, unavoidable.

Bernard Williams (1985, Ch. 9) makes a related point in his discussion of 'Relativism and Reflection'. He draws attention to the 'growth of reflective conscious-ness' which has typified the modern world over the past century or two: 'the urge to reflective understanding of society and our activities goes deeper and is more widely spread in modern society than it has ever been before' (1985, p. 163). Williams argues that

> there is no route back from reflectiveness. I do not mean that nothing can lead to its reduction; both personally and socially, many things can. But there is no *route* back, no way in which we can consciously take ourselves back from it.
> (pp. 163–4).

This line of argument gives further support to Raz's view that we live in an autonomy-supporting society and cannot help seeing our well-being as involving autonomy. It enables him to be able to defend autonomy in the stronger as well as in the weaker sense.

Before we leave this section, one or two further points about Callan's rejected arguments for autonomy, in the light of our discussion of Raz. The first argument was that autonomy is instrumental to happiness. Is Callan right to deny this? If we take happiness as equivalent to personal well-being, then Callan may indeed be right if he is making a universal claim about all human beings. But it still may be true *for us*—that is, in our kind of society—that autonomy is broadly necessary for well-being. (Agreed, this would not make it instrumental, necessarily). Part of Callan's objection to the first argument, noted above, is that a return to a tradition-directed society is a feasible option for us. But in the light of Williams' remark about reflectiveness, is this so?

In the course of his objection to the second argument—from the alleged absence of ethical experts—Callan says that it would be arbitrary for educators to lead children towards autonomy. But in the light of what has been said, would it be? If their flourishing demands this, is this not reason enough?

COMMUNITIES NOT FAVOURING AUTONOMY

I turn, finally, to the education of children from minorities living in the midst of an autonomy-supporting society like our own which do not themselves favour autonomy. Examples would be some religious communities, whether of Christian, Muslim or other persuasions, whose members are not encouraged critically to reflect on the basic assumptions of their belief systems. Should the autonomy aim be imposed on children in these communities?

We have seen that personal well-being is not always served by autonomy. This is true of tradition-directed societies. Could it be argued that children's well-being within the minority communities in question is better served by a non-autonomous upbringing? This is an argument which may lie behind demands for separate schooling. (There can also be other arguments for separate schooling. Some Afro-Caribbean children in the UK, it has been urged, may gain in confidence if educated away from white children, to whom they are often made to feel inferior.)

This argument does not work if children are going to spend their life, at least partly, within the wider open society as well as within their community. Here the autonomy aim still stands. Suppose, though, they are brought up wholly within their community: they can then hope, it may be said, to lead a flourishing life without being autonomous.

But there is an important difference between them and children brought up in a tradition-directed society, *not* within an open society. In the latter, their educators have no awareness of any alternative way of life. But in a minority community there *is* this awareness. This means that educators and other community leaders have to take steps to keep children within the fold, to prevent their being influenced by the values of the wider society. This means that forms of indoctrination may be used, aimed at a deliberate sequestration from the wider society and a deliberate restriction of attention to the values and traditions of the community.

How might this be justified? Can it be justified in terms of the children's well-being? But might it not have been better for them not to be indoctrinated but to be brought up as autonomous persons? Does the recourse to indoctrination not suggest that if the child could choose between the values of the closed and of the open society he might well choose the latter? The community leaders might appeal here to internal religious arguments that personal well-being is only possible via the religious belief in question. Things tend to get complicated at this point: there is usually no short way of settling disputes on this topic.

But even if it is difficult to show quite conclusively that a child's flourishing *cannot* depend on his being indoctrinated into a set of religious beliefs, does this imply that the community leaders should be left alone to indoctrinate? I do not see how it does. No one—and this includes the community leaders—would want to say that *anyone* has the right to bring up a child according to their own conception of human flourishing, whatever form this may take, and however convinced they are about the truth and unassailability of their conception, and willing to back up their position by acres of theological or other argument. A fundamentalist Christian, for instance, would not readily allow that a true believer of some other faith or a homespun ideologist of more idiosyncratic views had the right to impose his own conception of the good on children in his, the Christian's, community. Why, then, does the Christian think *he* has the right to do this? If he appeals to the truth and unassailability of his beliefs and to the inexhaustible arsenal of arguments to support them, he is in no different position from his opponent, for the latter will do exactly the same.

In an autonomy-supporting society *all* children must be protected against true believers who wish to impose on them a non-autonomous conception of the good life. How this is done is a further question. It does not necessarily mean open conflict between different cultural groups. Consideration for the integrity of the child's psychological development is enough on its own to point to the desirability of gentler methods.

NOTE

This chapter is an edited version of Chapter 6 of my book *Education and the Good Life: Beyond the National Curriculum*, London: Kogan Page (1990)

REFERENCES

Callan, E. (1988) *Autonomy and Schooling*. Kingston and Montreal: McGill-Queen's University Press.
Gray, J. (1983) *Mill on Liberty: A Defence*. London: Routledge & Kegan Paul.
Lindley, R. (1986) *Autonomy*. London: Macmillan.
Raz, J. (1986) *The Morality of Freedom*. Oxford: The Clarendon Press.
White, J. (1982) *The Aims of Education Restated*. London: Routledge & Kegan Paul.
Williams, B. (1985) *Ethics and the Limits of Philosophy*. London: Fontana.

Chapter 9

Censorship and Schooling

Robin Barrow

INTRODUCTION

Events in Tiananmen Square in 1989 and the case of Salman Rushdie's novel *The Satanic Verses* bring it home to us, if we needed reminding, that the issues of censorship and freedom of expression are very live ones. But at the same time as these dramatic political events are taking place, more familiar, but no less worrying, examples can be found in the schooling system. The West Vancouver Branch of the British Columbia Federation of English Teachers has recently resolved not to teach Shakespeare's *Merchant of Venice* on the grounds that it is racialist; elsewhere in Canada Jim Keegstra has been found guilty of wilfully promoting hatred against Jews, for arguing that the familiar story of the Nazi treatment of Jews is substantially incorrect, is in fact a Jewish plot (Bercuson and Wertheimer, 1985). In the United States creationists still seek to prevent the teaching of the theory of evolution, often with success. In certain school districts in Britain, books are unashamedly vetted and censored by political criteria. Censorship, which we perhaps tend to think of as a feature of other more repressive societies, is part of our everyday lives.

But, more than this, it is astonishing how 'legitimate' it has become, in cultures that perceive themselves as champions of liberty, to overtly call for the suppression of unpalatable truths. For example, in relation to a university professor who claims to have evidence that suggests certain innate racial differences between Indians, whites, and blacks, Ivor Goodson, of the University of Western Ontario, recently asserted, without qualm or argument, that academically sound science was not enough: one must produce socially acceptable science as well.[1] By this, Goodson means that one must not say things that might upset certain people or lead to social unrest, even if they are true.

In this chapter, I shall argue that censorship is never acceptable. More particularly, I shall suggest that Mill's classic argument in the fourth chapter of the essay *On Liberty* is entirely sound, noting in particular his point that it is a question of all or nothing here, and the fact that the entire argument is essentially an educational one. My conclusion will thus be that any kind of censorship in schools (which is the focus of this chapter) is morally repugnant.

CENSORSHIP AND SELECTION

There are various forms of censorship, and it is important to recognize as much, since how effective they may be, how easily they may be combated, and possibly even how objectionable they are, may vary. A reasonable basic categorization is provided by Roger Scruton, who distinguishes between (i) preventive censorship, where the state prevents the publication of offending material, (ii) punitive censorship, where publication is followed by legal prosecution, (iii) indirect control through 'responsible but autonomous bodies, such as the churches, and the Press Council, which have no legal, but some coercive power', (iv) indirect control through private libel actions, and (v) 'self-imposed censorship', referring to a decision not to publish made in the light of a personal judgement on what is socially and politically acceptable (Scruton, 1982).

One might, I think, argue that it is misleading and unhelpful to label the last 'censorship'. If I decide not to publish a book because I fear prosecution by the state or by an individual, then surely it is censorship of the second or fourth kind that is in question (and is incidentally achieving its purpose). If, on the other hand, I decide not to publish something simply because I think it may upset certain people, I am certainly not being censored by any external agency, and it is highly misleading to refer to self-censorship. For censorship is, by definition, a type of external coercion. Its analogous use in relation to the self only has plausibility in cases where we imagine a divided self. You censor me, if in some way you control my expression against my will. You do not 'censor' me, if my affection for you causes me not to say something hurtful. By extension, perhaps, I 'censor' myself, if, reluctantly, against my will in some respect, I bow down to some consideration that I cannot overcome, combat or get around. Thus, perhaps, it may be said that I 'censor' my remarks if I fear that the drunken lout in the corner will kill me should I utter them. But, if I decide that I will not say that I love you, because I fear that you might be embarrassed, angry or hurt, or because I think that I may look foolish, then in no recognizable sense am I 'censoring' myself. (If this attempt to deny that self-censorship is a form of censorship is found unconvincing, I shall simply observe that this form of censorship is legitimate, and I shall pay no further attention to it.)

Conversely, a curious feature of Scruton's typology is that he does not include the very common form of censorship that we associate with schools. For, very clearly, control of, editing of, and selection of material in schools may be censorship. Nor is it reasonable to equate this kind of control with the third type of censorship listed. The Press Council sets its standards and makes its decisions. This body has effective or *de facto* power over journalists, such that, for fear of their standing and job security, they will be strongly disinclined to say or write certain things. It is a straightforward example of institutional coercion. This is quite distinct from the systematic cultivation of, or exclusion of, some expressions of thought rather than others. For schools do not intimidate teachers into purveying some expression of thought rather than others, as, subtly, the Press Council, the Church, or the BMA intimidate their members (and as, indeed, the Teachers' Federation may). Rather, schools, by the agency of teachers, may, possibly unconsciously but nonetheless effectively, censor the expression of certain thoughts.[2]

At this point a distinction needs to be drawn between censorship and the broader term, selection. For, obviously, schools do, necessarily will continue to, and arguably should select material for study. How does one distinguish between selection and censorship in a case where, broadly speaking, there is little or no chance of restitution or compensation for what is not selected? There are, of course, differences of degree and exclusiveness between censorship and the selection of school materials. The ubiquity of *David Copperfield* and the absence of *Last Exit to Brooklyn* on most English syllabuses represents a less total control than the suppression of *Doctor Zhivago* in the Soviet Union for many years did. However, it is surely not because the latter constitutes a more effective and wide-ranging instance of control that we unhesitatingly classify it as censorship, in contrast to the limited *de facto* control of reading material in the former case.

We classify the suppression of *Doctor Zhivago* as censorship because, while extent and degree may feature in the concept, its essence is to be found in the idea of control being exercised according to criteria of ideological acceptability, rather than criteria that are peculiar and appropriate to the activity in question. Comedians weeding out their jokes by reference to what is going to be funny to their audience, even if the task is done by the theatre management, are not being censored. Editors who strike out arguments on the grounds that they are inapposite to the thesis being presented are not censoring. Censorship comes into play when the grounds of suppression and alteration change from being integral to the activity to being extraneous to it. The editor who strikes out an argument because it will offend his readers is censoring, because offence to readers is not a criterion of poor argument in the way that material that is not funny to a particular audience is a criterion of poor comedy. Thus, the management that will allow no mother-in-law jokes as a matter of principle is censoring, since many audiences will find some such jokes amusing.

It follows that schools are not guilty of censorship in so far as their selection of material is based on educational criteria, but that they are guilty of censorship in so far as they select material for wider political or ideological reasons. The systematic rejection of the works of James Joyce from the syllabus on the grounds that they are incomprehensible to the age group in question would, if the grounds were correct, be legitimate; and such selection would not constitute censorship even if the grounds were false and the decision therefore inapposite. On the other hand, the rejection of a history textbook because it involved a Marxist analysis that we think politically objectionable would be censorship. If it so happened that the intellectual community at large regarded Marxism as a ridiculous and incoherent doctrine, then one would be justified in ignoring it in the school curriculum. We would still not be justified in censoring the expression of Marxist views in the wider community, for reasons that will be spelt out in the next section. But, even if we turn out to be wrong in our estimate of Marxism, at the time that we make this judgement about its incoherence, we would be justified in ignoring it in schools, because we have educational grounds for so doing. Consequently, a question such as whether excluding creationist texts from the study of evolution constitutes censorship is fundamentally a question of whether creationism constitutes good science. It is because we believe that it manifestly does not, that in this case we need not fear the taunt of censorship.

FREEDOM OF EXPRESSION

Selection of material, I have suggested, is not necessarily censorship, and may be not only justifiable but required on educational grounds. However, there is also a great deal of attempted censorship of one sort or another in respect of the school curriculum, and one possible contributory factor to this is worth remarking on. Many attempts at censorship are clearly based upon the alleged psychological offensiveness of particular materials to various persons, rather than upon any claim about other kinds of harm they might cause. That is to say, we are often enjoined to censor something to avoid individual upset rather than to avoid bloodshed, loss of job, or other material disadvantage. That is all very well, but, at the same time, an era of heightened consciousness, such as we live in, is by definition an era of heightened sensitivity. Consequently, part of today's reality is that the utilitarian criterion of harm, when it refers to psychological offensiveness, is becoming less functional. Given a proliferation of such things as feminist, class and multicultural perspectives, there is very little that cannot be said to be harmful, in the sense of offensive, to some individual or group somewhere.

So what are we to say to this? Are we, for instance, to be moved by appeals to outlaw offensive language? We are to say again what John Stuart Mill has already so eloquently said. We are to recall his four-part argument that inclines us to recognize 'the necessity to the mental well being of mankind (on which all their other well being depends) of freedom of opinion, and freedom of the expression of opinion' (1968, p. 111). And, above all, we are to consider again how 'strange it is, that men should admit the validity of the arguments for free discussion, but object to their being pushed to an extreme; not seeing that unless the reasons are good for an extreme case, they are not good for any case' (*ibid.*, p. 83). Mill's point, in brief, is that since the argument for freedom of expression is not couched in terms of the advantage gained from particular acts of free expression, nor in terms of the overall gain in particular advantages from a policy of free expression, but in terms of the overall gain from having a hard and fast rule on the subject, it cannot make sense to allow of exceptions. I wish to argue similarly that censorship can never be justified. But even if one were to present a weaker thesis, the criterion of offensiveness would be a poor one to use. For there is no substance at all in an argument of the type 'we shouldn't censor unless the material is offensive', when what is offensive is a matter of who takes offence, rather than a matter of an agreed set of objectionable issues. Such a principle, quite apart from other considerations, would be unworkable in such circumstances.

We need to stress that hurt feelings, including the violent, shuddering, repulsion that, for example, Jews must feel if jokes are made about concentration camps, are neither here nor there in respect of argument about censorship. Mill's whole argument, as is well known, is that on grounds of utility, while certain actions may have to be disallowed, opinions never can be. The utility of this approach is no less real because it is long term. The reasoning behind it, one may suppose, is that certain actions are indisputably painful or harmful. Only the worst kind of philosopher could seriously maintain that a world in which individuals are free to mug, maim and rob, should they feel so inclined, might suit some people, and hence, perhaps, promote the general happiness. But the realm of opinion, however strongly we may feel, is not like that. However much we may be hurt by an idea, it is conceivable that we might not have been. Thus, even as we argue that the free expression of ideas is ultimately for the general good (see below), we have it in our power to minimize the potential pain caused by expressing certain opinions by altering our attitudes, and hence ceasing to take offence. This is an option that is not realistically open to us in respect of physical pain, to the same degree.[3]

For those who are not concerned with preserving the coherence of Mill's utilitarianism the situation is simple. The issue becomes straightforwardly one of truth and developing the human mind. We have to allow complete free expression of ideas, because (i) we have no right to claim the infallibility to declare an opinion false, (ii) no opinion is such that, even when wrong, its existence does not contribute to sharpening our focus on truth, (iii) the truths that we have will become formulae, if not kept alive by contrary argument, and (iv) the very nature of our truths changes if deprived of vitality: the dogma of the Christian church today is substantively different in kind from the vital faith of the early martyrs. Readers will forgive me if I do not elaborate on these well known, and surely in themselves self-evident, truths. It just is the case that censorship, any censorship, implies that we know for certain what is true, which nobody with philosophical acumen and historical awareness would want to say. It just is the case that our overall grasp of the truth cannot advance without challenge and interplay of ideas. It just is the case that unchallenged truth becomes dull (and dangerous) dogma. It just is the case that it ossifies into a different creed.[4]

The only way to challenge this position is to argue that the truth is not supremely important, that the world will not in the long run be happier for respecting the search for truth, and that human minds do not need to be developed as much as some incompatible goals, such as a certain kind of political stability, need to be achieved.[5]

CENSORSHIP IN SCHOOLS

As I have noted, Mill's general argument is in fact an educational one. As he says at one point, 'Not that it is solely, or chiefly, to form great thinkers, that freedom of thinking is required. On the contrary, it is as much and even more indispensable to enable average human beings to attain the mental stature which they are capable of' (1968, p. 94). And, certainly, schools, being essentially in the business of education, have to accept the argument. Even if Mill has overrated truth and underrated human happiness, for example, strange as that would be, the business of schools is not to compensate for, or take partisan positions on, various social ills (cf. Barrow, 1981). It is to develop the mind and cultivate understanding; it is conceptually committed to the pursuit of truth. To that end, in principle, any expression should be legitimate, even if it be offensive, contingently, to particular persons. To refrain from examining and questioning the grounds of religious belief, because some students are committed to such belief and do not feel comfortable with its being questioned, would be, by definition, anti-educational. Only if we were prepared to set ourselves up as infallible could we legitimately distinguish between this case and others that allegedly involve false doctrine. As I have said, we may reasonably decide not to teach creationism, because we have to select and we think that it is poor science. But that is not to say that we can reasonably forbid discussion of creationism, should it arise, on these grounds, still less on any ideological grounds.

We may conclude at once that a large number of interventions in the school curriculum constitute censorship and as such are morally and educationally offensive. Those who systematically censor books on feminist, anti-racialist, and other ideological grounds are to be deplored. Let us spell it out bluntly: it does not, in the final analysis, matter whether Shakespeare denigrates Jews, or Enid Blyton's Noddy demeans blacks; the minds of those who avoid facing up to such works on principle are a far greater threat to human well-being and to truth.

However, this cannot mean that anything goes, because a selection has to be made. There is evidence that, if we exclude blatantly political interventions such as are to be found in certain London education authorities, censorship is most commonly sought, at least by parents, in respect of (in descending order of importance): obscene language, sexual references, religious ideas, vulgarity, violence, inappropriate materials and moral values (cf. Davis, 1979). But distinctions need to be drawn here: obscene language is a matter of manners, and seeking to curb it amongst children need be no more a matter of censorship than demanding that feet or noses be wiped. If, however, books make use of obscene language as an integral part of what is otherwise educationally appropriate, there can be no objection. Sexual references, religious ideas and moral values are precisely the areas where freedom is most needed, they being highly complex and contentious areas, and blind faith being the antithesis of an educated position. 'Inappropriate materials' may refer either to educationally or ideologically inappropriate materials, and, consequently, may be either acceptable or unacceptable. The portrayal of vulgarity and violence, as with obscene language, may be undesirable, but cannot constitute a ground for rejecting an otherwise educationally desirable book.

It seems reasonable to conclude from the evidence that many instances of censorship in schools are not the result of any calculated policy, but rather the response that schools (particularly head teachers) make to aggressive parental complaints in order to avoid further trouble. Not unrelatedly, a number of commentators have argued that the situation would be markedly improved if schools were to accept and publicize a clear set of criteria for the selection of books and materials, in the light of which particular cases could be judged. There is some evidence both that such guidelines diminish the number of censorship problems that arise (cf. Olsen, 1974), and lead to a less restrictive policy on the part of librarians (cf. Pope, 1979). But, of course, in the end that is neither here nor there: what matters is that educational criteria only should be used—that is to say, criteria based on what is relevant to the development of the human mind and what we know about various stages of understanding. In other words, the issue is straightforwardly a matter of distinguishing between education and socialization.

The above argument against any censorship of school materials is, if accepted, certainly significant in its practical implications. But it should not be confused with the claim that teachers should be free to say anything. It does not, for example, follow from anything that I have said that I would have to allow Keegstra to teach.[6] I would allow him to speak and publish, and, by the argument, it is deplorable that he should be prevented from doing so (as well as, perhaps, counterproductive). But I do not have to let him teach, because there are very good grounds for saying he is a bad teacher. At the time of his trial, it must be admitted, the defence put forward the contrary case that he was a good teacher. But it did so by trading on the North American fixation with the fallacious idea that going through various motions makes one a good teacher (cf. Barrow, 1990). According to that way of looking at things, one is a good teacher in so far as one controls one's class in certain particular ways, engages in particular types of interpersonal communication, and adopts a number of attested teaching strategies. For all I know, Keegstra is a good teacher in this sense. But good teaching must be defined at least partly by reference to one's capacity to communicate sound understanding. Keegstra was a bad teacher because he is a teacher of history, yet he apparently cannot present, let alone appreciate, the overwhelming evidence for the standard account of events surrounding the Second World War. The fact that we find the evidence overwhelming does not, indeed, make the standard account necessarily true. It may be that future generations will laugh at me for accepting this view and acquit Keegstra of, at any rate, intellectual incompetence, but academic appointments are necessarily made by reference to the current standards of knowledge. By those standards Keegstra is an ignorant historian. He can speak, but he cannot be respected as an historian. And we are entitled to refuse to appoint a bad historian to the post of teacher of history.

It is true that selection, as well as censorship, may contribute to indoctrination (an issue considered in other chapters in this volume). Neither are to be confused with it, but rigorous censorship is obviously likely, may perhaps even be contingently necessary, to achieve successful indoctrination. On that ground alone, one has pragmatic grounds for objecting to censorship in schools, even if one is not convinced by Mill's argument. But selection of material on educational grounds, while it may conceivably make any attempt at indoctrination slightly easier to achieve, does not constitute the threat to open discussion that censorship does. In the first place, as I have said, to focus on a limited range of arguments as a result of selection is not to ban consideration of ideas and arguments that may arise. In the second place, to argue that certain works are of more educational value than others is to imply nothing about the value of the latter in other respects. In the third place, since by definition censorship involves suppressing works on ideological grounds, it involves a refusal to consider a particular perspective. By contrast, selection on educational criteria need not rule out any perspective (although in practice one concedes it may ignore some).

It may be suggested that all thought is ideological, and that therefore the educational criteria of selection involve an ideological bias as much as the more blatantly political censorship of books does. Certainly the word 'ideological' can be used so broadly as to cover both cases. And certainly it may be the case that, specifically, our conception of education is tied up with our wider frame of values and understanding, which may owe something, perhaps a lot, to our particular cultural history. Nonetheless, there seems a very clear difference between saying 'We in this society have reason to believe that these materials are not readily comprehensible to children of a certain age, and that this mode of argument is radically flawed, and we therefore do not consider it appropriate to spend limited educational time on them', and saying 'Since this book espouses a view of the world that we do not like we shall ban it.' It is the latter kind of approach that I refer to as 'ideological'.

It should also be noted that the banning of, say, *The Merchant of Venice* as a matter of principle is to be distinguished from judicious selection in particular cases. If a teacher has reason to think that reading the play with his students will incite racial animosity or cause great upset to some, he might very reasonably select a different play with the same educational value for his purposes. That is, again, clearly quite different from maintaining that nobody ought to be allowed to read the play on the grounds that it is offensive. It is not necessarily offensive, and even if it were that would not constitute grounds for censoring it. It may, however, sometimes prove educationally unsuitable to make use of the play.

CONCLUSION

My conclusion, then, is that freedom of expression should be absolute. Utilitarians will argue that such absolute freedom is necessary for the ultimate well-being of mankind, and I believe that to be a very plausible argument. But others need only to value truth itself to see that freedom of expression must be absolute. To attempt to set any limits on it is, by implication, to presume the one thing that we know not to be true: namely, that we can be logically, as opposed to psychologically, certain of anything. (I discount analytic truths, which are not material to the present argument.) Censorship, being a limitation of freedom of expression, is therefore never justified. In schools one has to select, and one may legitimately do that on educational grounds, which encompass what we believe about the development of children, how they learn, and what we are trying to achieve in the name of education. There is nothing wrong, therefore, with making the judgement that library funds should not be spent on pornography or obscene literature, or that it would be wiser to study this textbook than that. There may be nothing wrong either with schools preferring one textbook to another on grounds such as that it is less ethnocentric, less inclined to ignore the role of women, or less explicitly sexual. But what is quite unacceptable is a decision systematically to suppress otherwise educationally suitable material simply because it is judged by some to be offensive.

NOTES

(1)   Cf. Ivor Goodson, 'Science can't be divorced from social responsibility', *London Free Press*, 7 February 1989. Goodson's remarks were directed against Dr Philippe Rushton, a psychology professor at the University of Western Ontario.

(2)   Another potential distinction that needs to be mentioned, although I shall not explore it here, is between censorship in 'normal' circumstances, and censorship in time of, for example, war. It may be possible to argue that a government edict making the publication of certain information illegal in time of war does not constitute censorship (or introduces an importantly distinct conception of censorship). But, in any case, conclusions drawn in the context of this chapter are not intended necessarily to apply to a state of war.

(3)   What is true is that Mill's account does not offer any clear criteria for distinguishing between incitement to act and support for or argument about the merits of an action. He tells us plainly enough that 'even opinions lose their immunity when the circumstances in which they are expressed are such as to constitute their expression a positive instigation to some mischievous act' (1968, p. 114), but does not attempt to explain how we distinguish between, say, an argument for what some would call a racist viewpoint and a speech that leads directly to a lynching. There is a case for saying that such a distinction does not need to be drawn: it is those who are incited to lynch who should be prevented from acting, rather than those who speak in ways that instigate the desire so to act. Most readers will probably reject that position, in which case it is true that any such view as I present in the

text ultimately needs further consideration of this issue, amongst others. For the present, I will rest content with stressing (a) that the argument is, at the least, that any utterance is permissible, however offensive, provided that it does not directly engender unacceptable action, and (b) that, in the particular context of censorship and schools, the argument is that no book or opinion should be suppressed on any but educational grounds.

(4) It has been argued by, for example, H. J. McCloskey that the argument 'rests on very questionable assumptions; and it purports to establish much more than it can and does' (1971, p. 119). In particular he makes the point that not all silencing of discussion is an assumption of infallibility. In defending Mill against this and similar criticisms Gray (1983) makes the convincing point that 'these traditional criticisms neglect the point . . . that liberty of thought and expression is valuable, not just instrumentally as a means to the discovery and propagation of truth, but non-instrumentally, as a condition of that rationality and vitality of belief which he conceives of as a characteristic feature of a free man' (p. 107).

(5) Something also needs to be said about libel, if only because of the recent spate of libel trials accompanied by astonishingly high awards for damages in Britain. On the face of it the idea that one should be free to calumniate and vilify others is counter-intuitive. Surely there ought to be some restriction on my freedom to spread damaging lies about another? Consistently with my argument above, I do not think so. I do not dispute the morally objectionable nature of such activity nor underestimate its potential damage to individuals. But it remains the case that to adopt a law against libel is to risk suppressing the truth, is to inhibit full understanding of what is true, is to allow traditional assumptions (in this case popular estimates of individuals) to ossify, and thence to change their nature. In the long run, in the interests of truth, we must be free to lie about each other.

(6) See above, p. 94.

REFERENCES

Barrow, R. (1981) *The Philosophy of Schooling*. Brighton: Wheatsheaf.
Barrow, R. (1990) *Understanding Skills: Thinking, Feeling and Caring*. London and Ontario: Althouse Press.
Bercuson, D. and Wertheimer D. (1985) *The Trust Betrayed: The Keegstra Affair*. Toronto: Althopuse Press.
Davis, J. E. (ed.) (1979) *Dealing with Censorship*. Urbana, IL: National Council of Teachers of English.
Gray, J. (1983) *Mill on Liberty: A Defence*. London: Routledge & Kegan Paul.
McCloskey, H. J. (1971) *John Stuart Mill: A Critical Study*. London: Macmillan.
Mill, J. S. (1968) *On Liberty*, ed., A.D. Lindsay. London: Dent.
Olsen, T. (1974) Censorship and selection. *Journal of Reading*, **March**, 502–3.
Pope, M. (1979) *Sex and the Undecided Librarian*. Metuchen, NJ: Scarecrow Press.
Scruton, R. (1982) *A Dictionary of Political Thought*. London: Macmillan

Name Index